A Mind at Peace

Christopher O. Blum and Joshua P. Hochschild

A Mind at Peace

Reclaiming an Ordered Soul
in the Age of Distraction

SOPHIA INSTITUTE PRESS
Manchester, New Hampshire

Sophia Institute Press
Box 5284, Manchester, NH 03108
1-800-888-9344

www.SophiaInstitute.com

Sophia Institute Press® is a registered trademark of Sophia Institute.

Library of Congress Cataloging-in-Publication Data

Names: Blum, Christopher Olaf, 1969- author.
Title: A mind at peace : reclaiming an ordered soul in the age of distraction / Christopher O. Blum, Joshua P. Hochschild.
Description: Manchester, New Hampshire : Sophia Institute Press, 2017. | Includes bibliographical references.
Identifiers: LCCN 2017026173 | ISBN 9781622823819 (pbk. : alk. paper)
Subjects: LCSH: Christian life. | Peace of mind—Religious aspects—Christianity. | Well-being—Religious aspects—Christianity. | Catholic Church—Doctrines.
Classification: LCC BV4501.3 .B585 2017 | DDC 248.4/82—dc23 LC record available at https://lccn.loc.gov/2017026173

First printing

A Prayer of St. Augustine

Breathe in me, O Holy Spirit, that my thoughts may all be holy.
Act in me, O Holy Spirit, that my work, too, may be holy.
Draw my heart, O Holy Spirit, that I love but what is holy.
Strengthen me, O Holy Spirit, to defend all that is holy.
Guard me, then, O Holy Spirit, that I always may be holy. Amen.

Contents

Part III: Thinking Well

Foreword

Lord, Jesus, may I know myself and may I know You.

—St. Augustine

Saint Augustine famously defined *peace* as "the tranquility of order." We all intuit the truth of that statement. We know that if we ourselves are properly ordered—in the various dimensions of our lives, in our union of body and soul, of intellect, will, and passions—then we will be at peace, no matter the difficulties around us. By the same token, we know that if we lack that interior order—if we are at odds with ourselves—then no amount of external order can bring us peace.

But we live in a schizophrenic culture. As much as we might want that peace, we still desire the world's distractions. We love the gifts of the digital age: "Big Data," connectivity, constant streaming, and so forth—even as we sense a need for quiet, for relief from information and communication overload. We want both the promises of the digital age and the habit of recollection ("mindfulness," as it is now fashionable to say). It is increasingly clear how difficult it is to have both—to be at once digitalized and recollected.

A Mind at Peace

Our tools have gotten in the way. Of course, all tools get in the way. While you use a hammer, you cannot shake hands. When you saw wood, you cannot write a letter. But what we experience now is different. Our tools—the new, digital technologies—do not just get in *our* way but get in the way of our *selves*. The insertion of digital technology into every sphere of life disconnects us not just from this thing or that but from our very selves. To think, reason, see, and touch have all taken on new meaning.

Indeed, our humanity now seems proportioned to technology. The smartphone was initially designed to the human hand—to fit its size, shape, and motion. Now we fit ourselves to our digital devices. They have become the measure. We bring them everywhere (to work, in the car, on the plane, on the train ...) and turn to them for every need ("There's an app for that"). We even describe ourselves in their terms. People "outsource" their memory and "process" rather than think. Human sight, meant to gaze on God's creation, now looks at everything through a screen. For many people the sense of touch is engaged most of all on a touch pad.

Salvation, on the other hand, is proportioned to our humanity. *And the Word became flesh and dwelt among us* (John 1:14). God did not demand that we rise to His level. He proportioned Himself to us, so that we mere creatures can receive His grace and truth. Thus, the language of salvation is that of the human senses: *Hear, O Israel! . . . Taste and see the goodness of the Lord! . . . Behold, the Lamb of God! . . . Take and eat. . . .* The Church's sacramental economy likewise depends on simple human acts: pouring water, anointing with oil, eating bread, drinking wine, speaking vows.

The psalmist addresses God as *salutare vultus mei*—"the Savior of my face" (Ps. 42:6, 12; 43:5). That phrase summarizes things neatly. To be human means to have a face—to be capable of relationships, and ultimately of beholding God's glory. Sin robs us of that. It turns us inward, away from others—in effect, without a face. We need to be restored to ourselves—to "save face."

Today's technology has, in a sense, robbed us of our face, has disconnected us from ourselves. Our very faces have disappeared behind screens. In this regard, too, God is *the Savior of my face*. When our tools get in our way and we forget what it means to be human, God can restore us to ourselves.

This is not a book about technology. It is a book about being restored to ourselves and thus finding peace. There are many good books on the dangers of technology. This book is different in both its depth and its practicality. Our crisis calls for sound philosophy, a clear explanation of human nature—so that we can reacquaint ourselves with ourselves. It is not enough to observe that technology can be bad for us. We must also know the good: the good that we are and what is good for us. The crisis likewise calls for theology. We have been created by God and for God—and He alone restores us. Finally, the crisis calls for practical advice—so that the philosophy and theology do not remain theoretical but gain traction in our lives.

Christopher Blum and Joshua Hochschild have woven these elements together in this powerful little book. It is deep in the wisdom of what it means to be human, clear in God's power to save, and simple in tactics for moving forward. It is not primarily about "disconnecting" from our devices but about reconnecting with God and therefore with ourselves. May its readers be many, and may it help them come to know the peace He promised.

—Father Paul Scalia
Corpus Christi, 2017

Introduction

Have you ever regretted sending an e-mail, a text, or a post? Have you recently forgotten an appointment that a year or two ago you would have had no difficulty remembering? Do you catch your mind wandering when you should be attending carefully to the task, or the person, right in front of you?

What about the way you have been spending your time? Is it difficult to refrain from checking your phone or e-mail every several minutes? Are you uncomfortable being alone and quick to look for relief from boredom? Do you find yourself browsing websites or trying to keep up with the latest news? Do you fall into binge-watching television shows, or playing just one more round of a video game? Are you preoccupied with social media to the point of compulsively checking updates, statuses, and likes?

Are you more often ill at ease or anxious than in the past? Are you uncomfortable with your own thoughts? Do you feel unfocused, distracted, restless? Are you finding less joy in con-versation, reading, and prayer than you used to?

If you are answering many of these questions with a regretful yes, then know that you are not alone. And be consoled: there are remedies. It is possible to regain an ordered and peaceful mind, which thinks more clearly and attends more steadily. The saints and the wise can show you how; this book aims to make their counsel available to you.

The essential goodness of peace hardly needs to be vindi-cated in an age characterized by increasing anxiety. There is a growing chorus of concern about the influence of digital media on our habits of living, sensing, and thinking. In his bestseller *The Shallows: What the Internet Is Doing to Our Brains*, Nicho-las Carr frankly confessed, "I'm not thinking the way I used to think" and went on to lament his diminished ability to follow a complex argument or to enjoy a lengthy book.[1] A celebrated professor of technology studies, Sherry Turkle, has argued that our habits of using communications technology are making us "insecure, isolated, and lonely" and warned of our tendency to seek consolation in machines.[2] In *The World Beyond Your Head*, political theorist Matthew B. Crawford suggested that our age is passing through a "crisis of attention," the result of which is that we are losing our ability to act "according to settled pur-poses and ongoing projects" and instead coming under the in-fluence of powerful interests seeking to profit from our loss of

---

[1] Nicholas Carr, *The Shallows: What the Internet Is Doing to Our Brains* (New York: Norton, 2010), 5.

[2] Sherry Turkle, *Alone Together: Why We Expect More from Tech-nology and Less from Each Other* (New York: Basic Books, 2012), 157.

self-command.[3] Adam Gazzaley, a neuroscientist, and Larry D.
Rosen, a psychologist, have documented and analyzed the results
of using "ancient brains in a high-tech world": anxiety, boredom,
weakened memory, poor goal management, general loss of cognitive control.[4]

These authors and many others, writing from different disci-
plines and perspectives, have helped to assess the consequences
of the introduction of powerful new digital technologies into
some of the most intimate and significant parts of our lives. As
these technologies grow and change and further alter our social
environments, we can expect the trends they have noticed to
continue. Their general conclusion is undeniable: modern technology presents powerful challenges to our interior well-being.

Today we are less settled and more easily manipulated, more
often distracted, and more deeply worried than we were thirty
years ago. These are not healthy developments. The loss of our
mental and spiritual composure threatens all that is most important in our lives: our work, our ability to make decisions, our
self-knowledge, and our relationships with each other and with
God. It is increasingly clear that our habits of using technology
are contributing to interior suffering.[5] Something must be done,
but the remedy would not seem to be, for most of us, at any rate,

---

[3] Matthew B. Crawford, *The World Beyond Your Head: On Becoming
an Individual in an Age of Distraction* (New York: Farrar, Straus,
and Giroux, 2016), ix.

[4] Adam Gazzaley and Larry D. Rosen, *The Distracted Mind: Ancient Brains in a High-Tech World* (Cambridge/London: MIT Press,
2016).

[5] See the study by the American Psychological Association, *Stress
in America 2017: Technology and Social Media*, February 23, 2017,
apa.org.

as simple as turning off and dropping out. What we need is an approach to self-mastery that is deep enough and comprehensive enough to enable us to navigate the digital age while maintaining our peace within.

There have been a number of extraordinary revolutions in human communication through the centuries, and thus far, each of them has proved in the long run to have been permanent. We cannot imagine a world without the alphabet, or writing, or the printing press. Nor can many of us summon up a realistic sense of what life would be like in the absence of the kind of long-distance personal communication made possible by the telegraph and the telephone, or the public communication that the radio and the television gave to the twentieth century.

Many of us, however, can remember the world before personal computers, the Internet, and mobile phones. The current revolution in digital communication is at most thirty years old, and, in some respects—for instance, in the case of smartphones and social media—significantly younger than that. That this revolution will similarly be a permanent cultural shift seems certain. And it will be a cultural shift whose magnitude we cannot yet foresee.

This book is a guide for those who find themselves increasingly troubled and perplexed in the digital age that is upon us. It contains an ongoing engagement with the new digital technology but is primarily an examination of those qualities of character that we must cultivate in order to survive in the media-saturated environment in which we now live. This book is in the first place a reminder of what the human race has long known about how gently but persistently to lead to health our interior faculties of sensing, understanding, choosing, and rejoicing in the good and the true. This book is not an argument for retreat from the world

Introduction

as we find it, but a practical guide to recovering interior peace through wise choices and ordered activity.

It was once commonly known that the enjoyment of interior peace was the reward of virtuous living, a healthy and appropriately restrained sensory life, a clear mind able steadily to consider the causes of things in our changing world, and a heart often lifted to God. It is that perspective that has shaped the pages that follow. An everyday metaphor used by the apostle St. James captures our purpose: "The farmer waits for the precious fruit of the earth, being patient over it until it receives the early and the late rain. You also be patient. Establish your hearts, for the coming of the Lord is at hand" (James 5:7–8). Our great need today is to establish our hearts anew amidst the worries that beset our age. St. Francis de Sales taught that "the greatest evil that can happen to a soul" other than actual sin is to be gripped by anxiety. "If our heart is inwardly troubled and disturbed," he explained, "it loses both the strength necessary to maintain the virtues it acquired and the means to resist the temptations of the enemy."[6] This book, accordingly, is intended as a guide to the rediscovery of those aspects of the wisdom of the ages that can restore our souls to peace.

A Mind at Peace is the result of conversations — often carried out over e-mail — between two Catholic educators who have devoted their careers to making available to today's students the wisdom of the broad Catholic tradition of philosophical, theological, and spiritual reflection. Although we have never been at the same institution since leaving graduate school, our experiences of the challenges posed by contemporary culture

---

[6] St. Francis de Sales, *Introduction to the Devout Life*, trans. John K. Ryan (1950; New York: Image Books, 2003), 239.

have been similar. Those experiences have led to a shared conviction that the Catholic tradition of reflection offers principles for the discernment of culture that are of vital importance today.

This work is primarily devoted to reflection upon those principles. It is divided into three parts. The first treats the virtues by which we bring order to our exterior actions and to the appetites that spur us onward to act. The second discusses our sensory faculties, now more than ever besieged by the media. The third examines our deepest interior faculties of knowing and willing. Each chapter ends with a brief selection from Sacred Scripture or a spiritual classic, which is offered as an occasion for meditation or prayer, and then provides some questions for self-examination, which can be used to make practical, manageable, sustainable resolutions to carry us forward toward the enjoyment of interior peace.

Part I

Living Well

1

Self-Aware

I will praise thee; for I am fearfully and wonderfully made.
—Psalm 139:14, KJV

Peace is a presence. From Sacred Scripture, we learn that peace is a perfection, a gift from God, a positive, dynamic, and healthy state — either between people or within the soul. St. Augustine said that peace is the tranquility of order.[7] Peace is not an emptiness or an absence or a passive state, so much as it is repose within a state of activity. Order is the order *of* something, the right arrangement of something present and real. Even in political terms, it would be a mistake to think of peace as merely the lack of violent or destructive action. Real political peace is a dynamic harmony within and between states or nations. Peace is the presence of harmonious action.

We seek to address personal peace, especially peace in the mind, heart, and soul. This is a distinctly human challenge, and so we must start by reflecting upon what is distinctive about

---

[7] St. Augustine, *City of God* 19.13.

the human being. We have qualities all our own, and human fulfillment requires that we bring order to these qualities. In this sense, understanding true peace is like understanding true happiness or true freedom: it requires us to attend to the essential activity of human beings, and to how that activity can achieve its fulfillment or perfection.

Let us begin with what we are not. We are not machines. Robots have behavioral outputs that are entirely determined by mechanical and electrical inputs. While we sometimes use metaphors of machines to describe human activity, and metaphors of human activity to describe machines, we know that there is an essential difference between us and them. Artificial intelligence is at best an attempt to replicate the behavioral *effects* of human intelligence, not the thing itself. When we program a computer to learn something, or to speak, we have not created a living intelligence. The computer that knows and remembers is not really knowing and remembering. No matter how convincingly the robot speaks its message — "I love you" or "I don't want to die" — the fact that it is a robot means that we do not believe that it is a true message. We do not think that robots can express personal devotion, anxiety about mortality, or any other authentic human concern.

Unlike machines, we have feelings, emotions, and awareness of our environment. When humans seek peace, it is in large part these feelings, emotions, and different kinds of awareness that need discipline, coordination, and order. Without order, our attention is divided, distracted, confused, unreliable, and ineffective. With order, our attention is focused, directed, clear, trustworthy, and fruitful. Several later chapters will treat different levels of feelings and emotions, and how they can be ordered and directed most appropriately. Yet we are much more than our feelings. Just as we are not machines, so also are we not beasts. An ordered life is not a matter of instinct or behavioral conditioning. We must take responsibility for working to achieve the order of the soul that is true peace. We have agency, the power to act, and the responsibility to order our actions toward a known purpose. Unlike machines or other animals, then, we human creatures can speak of self-mastery or self-control. We make choices, we govern our activity, and we sense — even if we are also sometimes tempted to ignore it — a responsibility to do these things *well*.

This power, the power to choose and to act, is the key to achieving peace.

Philosophers say that we are rational animals, and theologians that we have been made in the image of God. Both statements can be elaborated at length, but fundamentally they make a common claim about what is distinctive to human life: we are unique in the natural world for knowingly governing our own actions, for having a share in intelligent providence. In short, unlike beasts or machines, we act with responsibility because we are aware of purposes.

This human spark, rationality, is more than the ability to theorize or to calculate; it is rational agency, the fundamentally human knowledge of intentional action. This human spark is, from a biblical perspective, a divine spark, an image of a perfect Intelligence and Will. By exercising our human agency to govern our actions, we actively participate in the divine agency governing the entire universe.

We are aware of what we do, and we take responsibility for what we do. We evaluate our fellow human beings according to whether they act well, that is, to the extent that their reason and will are properly employed. We fault a person for choosing what is wrong. We may pity a person for acting in ignorance. We criticize a person who lacks will power. And we praise someone who discerns and voluntarily pursues good ends. Even our legal system makes sense only to the extent that it seeks to determine the level of intelligence and freedom of our actions. A judge attempts to establish not merely the facts of an external behavior, but the agent's state of mind and intention as well.

We are and must be judges of action. We judge others' actions. Was he being generous or simply trying to manipulate me? Did that person strike me by accident or on purpose? And we judge our own actions. We deliberate about what we should do and how we should do it; we evaluate our motives and intentions; we ask forgiveness for our faults, and we confess our sins.

Peace is a perfection of human agency. We can achieve peace only through what we choose to do. Even the rich young man, who had everything, knew that he was missing the true happiness and peace that will come with eternal life, and accordingly he asked, "What must I do" (see Matt. 19:16). This book is about how to achieve the personal peace that comes from choosing and acting well, and so we will attend closely to ordering action. Happiness is not a matter simply of having good intentions, but of rightly understanding and responding well to our emotions, to our environment, and to other people. A highly functioning person is not someone who is merely nice or makes a positive difference in the world, but instead someone who can competently take stock of his situation, discern the actions available to him, and reliably choose the best.

A first necessary step, then, is to recall that actions can be chosen, that individual actions, and an extended life of action, are indeed the instruments of our peace. That is why we begin with this reflection on our awareness of ourselves as agents. We cannot achieve peace without remembering that each of us as human beings can understand and intend specific ends.

We must remember that we are agents. Perhaps this seems too obvious to bear repeating, but one modern source of disquiet, one common obstacle to peace, is a kind of forgetfulness of our agency, of our ability to act. There are ideas and influences that threaten to lull us into passivity. There are forces that disguise our sense of responsibility for action, that distract us from the obligation to act, or that tempt us to ignore the possibility of acting for a purpose.

One of the culprits is bad philosophy. It is common to blame relativism, the stance taken by those who protest that there is no such thing as truth, no such thing as right or wrong, and no way to judge an action as either good or bad. The wise have always held such a stance to be untenable. In the ancient world, just as today, the rebuttal was straightforward: does the relativist walk into the hole that he sees in front of him? No, of course not. Yet even people who would not embrace outright relativism might adhere to a subtler version, which holds that evaluations of human action are merely opinions as opposed to facts. In his classic essay *The Abolition of Man*, C. S. Lewis identified the danger of this soft relativism, which reduces judgments of value to expressions of subjective feeling and tools by which to influence other people.

Many cultural critics have identified ways in which modern mass culture feels like a condition in which human beings are treated as something other than authentic agents. The bureaucratic mind-set, the therapeutic mind-set, the consumerist mind-set: all, in their own ways, are descriptions of cultural patterns in which people are treated as objects to be manipulated, rather than as persons responsible for action. We laugh at exaggerated versions of this tendency, such as the lazy, superficial, numb residents of the *Axiom* spaceship in the animated film *Wall-E*, a film in which the robots are more truly agents in search of fulfillment than the people are. Yet we laugh with nervousness and perhaps shame, because we recognize ourselves in the depiction. It is an exaggeration of a real possibility. We can indeed become blind to our ability to act.

Sophisticated technology also has a way of obscuring our awareness of agency. Some technology truly empowers us by focusing or extending the range of our action. Yet it is common to observe that, once integrated into new patterns of life, we can feel shaped by our own machines.[8] A tool is something that requires skill and virtue to use well. Often, however, our technologies are not merely tools that strengthen our agency in this way, but are devices that substitute for skill and virtue by allowing us to achieve goals without effort and without a sense of responsibility. This feature of technology has long been observed, but it has been noticed in distinctive ways in the digital age. One of the most striking features of Sherry Turkle's research into the use of smartphones and social media is that, when asked to reflect, most people, especially young people, are able to recognize the bad habits, the unhealthy dynamics, and the selfishness and narcissism manifested in their use of digital technology, yet continue to act as they have grown accustomed to do. This is a classic sign of addiction, which is a crippling of agency, a pathological directing of one's freedom into a rut of compulsion. We know that some technology designers — of hardware interfaces, of games and other apps, even of social media — aim to induce addiction by drawing

---

[8] See Nicholas Carr, *The Glass Cage: How Our Computers Are Changing Us* (New York: Norton, 2014).

on cutting-edge neurological and psychological research to hook users on their products.

The first step in resisting and overcoming addiction is an honest self-awareness, as an agent responsible to other agents for doing what is good. The addict must recognize that the behavior is pathological and admit the need for help. The very awareness of the need for help is the first step toward the restoration of agency. The addict's awareness of a problem and sense of surrender (for instance, in a typical twelve-step recovery program) is an acknowledgment of a responsibility to a higher good or purpose, God Himself, who can help him to reorient his own actions.

It is widely known that Western countries, despite (or, more likely, because of) their high degree of comfort and wealth, have unusually high incidences of depression and other psychopathologies manifesting themselves in a sense of dissipation of the will or paralysis of action. From a theological perspective, it is plausible to assert that "the unnamed evil of our times" is the sin of acedia, or sloth, which is not mere laziness, but truly a kind of discouragement, torpor, or despair, a sense of purposelessness and powerlessness.[9] On Dante's Mount Purgatory, each of the seven deadly sins is purged with a prayer and a purifying punishment. The sin of those too slowly moved by love, those whose sense of agency has been degraded by acedia, is purified by a simple and primal action: running. By insistently doing something, by exerting the will, the soul is reminded of and strengthened in its power, restored in its zeal. It is at this level of Mount Purgatory

---

[9] For further reflection on this point, see Jean-Charles Nault, O.S.B., *The Noonday Devil: Acedia, The Unnamed Evil of Our Times* (San Francisco: Ignatius Press, 2015), and R.J. Snell: *Acedia and Its Discontents: Metaphysical Boredom in an Empire of Desire* (Kettering, OH: Angelico Press, 2015).

that Virgil explains to Dante the distinct power of the human soul, its true freedom:

> You have an inborn power, your reason, meant
> to gather every will to that first will,
> advising at the threshold of assent.
> This is the principle whereby a man
> takes merit in a good or evil love,
> gathering fruit and picking out the bran.[10]

Blessings on Those
Who Choose God's Way

Psalm 1

Blessed is the man who walks not in the counsel of
    the wicked,
Nor stands in the way of sinners, nor sits in the
    seat of scoffers;
But his delight is in the law of the LORD, and on
    his law he meditates day and night.
He is like a tree planted by streams of water,
That yields its fruit in due season, and its leaf does
    not wither.
In all that he does, he prospers.
The wicked are not so, but are like chaff which the
    wind drives away.

[10] Dante, *Purgatory*, canto XVIII, lines 61–66, trans. Anthony Esolen (New York: Modern Library, 2004), 195.

Therefore the wicked will not stand in the
    judgment,
Nor sinners in the congregation of the righteous;
For the Lord knows the way of the righteous,
But the way of the wicked will perish.

Questions for Reflection

• *In what kinds of activity am I most aware of myself as a fully
responsible, focused, and skilled agent, and most empowered
to act as my true self? Do I need to rededicate myself to these
activities?*

• *In what areas of my life am I prone to compulsive behavior,
tempted to ignore my agency, or inclined to shirk responsibility for my actions? Is there a pattern of my behavior that I
would be better off without?*

2

Pure of Heart

If there is joy in this world, it belongs to the pure of heart.

—Thomas à Kempis, *The Imitation of Christ* II.4

Life is a supreme good. God is his own life, and he has shared that life with us his creatures. As St. Paul memorably said, borrowing the words of an ancient poet, "In him we live and move and have our being" (Acts 17:28). The Son of God affirmed this solemn truth: "I came that they may have life, and have it abundantly" (John 10:10). Truly, Jesus "delighted in the sons of men" (Prov. 8:31), choosing certain men and women to be his close friends, and teaching and training them so that, as his mission drew to a close, he was able to invite them to share it as his fellow-laborers: "No longer do I call you servants, for the servant does not know what his master is doing; but I have called you friends, for all that I have heard from my Father I have made known to you" (John 15:15). The Lord's way of life was so ordinary, so touch-ingly human, so ungodlike, that it shocked and brought scandal to the undiscerning. "The Son of man came eating and drinking, and they say, 'Behold, a glutton and a drunkard, a friend of tax

A Mind at Peace

collectors and sinners!'" (Matt. 11:19). Yes, Jesus dined with Zacchaeus, wept for Lazarus, turned water into wine at Cana, blessed the little children who approached him, and solemnly affirmed the holiness of lifelong marriage between one man and one woman. The Lord of heaven and earth is the Lord of life.

Today, our confusion about such matters is acute. We are continually buffeted by the winds of contrary gospels: it is good for people to be able to end their own lives; it is good for people to be able to kill children in the womb; it is good for people to be able to marry whomsoever they will, for as long or as briefly as they choose. It is reassuring to note that this maelstrom of opinion has been swirling for the better part of a century, and has been opposed at every step by stalwart witnesses to truth. In 1939 the Anglican poet T. S. Eliot, reacting to the decision of the Church of England to accept contraception as a normal practice, surmised that "it would perhaps be more natural, as well as in better conformity to the Will of God, if there were more celibates and if those who were married had larger families."[11] Eliot's contemporary, Gabriel Marcel, warned that the twentieth century had witnessed "a work of systematic subversion which is no longer directed against revealed doctrines or principles hallowed by tradition, but against nature itself."[12] And above all, we recall the astonishing rejoinder to our permissive culture levied by a diminutive Albanian nun, from the rostrum of the Nobel award ceremony in 1979: abortion "is the greatest

[11] T. S. Eliot, "The Idea of a Christian Society" (1939), in *Christianity and Culture* (New York: Harcourt, 1977), 48.
[12] Gabriel Marcel, *Homo Viator: Introduction to the Metaphysics of Hope*, trans. Emma Craufurd and Paul Seaton (South Bend, IN: St. Augustine's Press, 2010), 87.

20

destroyer of peace today. Because if a mother can kill her own child — what is left for me to kill you and you kill me — there is nothing between."[13]

This is the proper context in which to understand the great and glorious virtue of temperance, the foundation stone of a just society and of interior peace, because it is the virtue by which the very springs of life in our bodies are protected and brought under the rule of reason and grace. Often thought of as self-control, temperance is a prerequisite to true freedom.

"A tranquil mind gives life to the flesh, but passion makes the bones rot" (Prov. 14:30). This bit of wisdom cuts deep. Here we see the essential unity of body and soul on display, as well as an indication of the different powers of the soul, the powers the philosophers will call the vegetative, the sensitive, and the rational. Life we have in common with the animals and the plants, and so it should not surprise us that some of our powers operate without our thinking about them and beyond our control. Just as plants photosynthesize, grow, and produce seeds according to their nature, and without choosing to, so also do we digest, grow, and produce seed, as it were, automatically. Where temperance comes in is at the level of our sensations, for like other animals, we find pleasure in eating and mating, even though the biological processes that underlie those pleasures and make them possible are outside of our conscious control. In other words, there is a difference between the powers of life in us and our appetite for the pleasures associated with their activities. We have no cause to doubt the difference. Plenty of people have desires that

---

[13] "Mother Teresa — Nobel Lecture," December 11, 1979, Nobel-Prize.org, http://www.nobelprize.org/nobel_prizes/peace/laureates/1979/teresa-lecture.html.

outstrip what is good for their biological powers; when they give in to those desires over and over again, then "passion makes the bones rot."

The virtue of temperance is a disposition to enjoy the pleasures that follow from the performance of these basic biological functions in the right way, at the right time, and for the right end. Like the other virtues we will discuss, temperance is a habit. Just like being able to swim the backstroke, or to ride a bike, or to read Latin, temperance is an ability that we gain above and beyond the powers we are born with. Our character is made up of our habits. The man or woman other people take us to be is the person who is inclined or apt to act in such and such a way, according to habit. To be human is to need habits, for our power to choose and to act extends very broadly: we can study aeronautic engineering or music theory, learn to dance or to fence, become generous or stingy, be compassionate or hardhearted, and so on. Among the various habits that we can gain, many relate to our minds directly, others to our bodies and their appetites. In the case of temperance, it is the twofold appetite for life that the habit governs: we cannot live without eating, and the human race cannot endure without reproducing, and so, like the other animals, we find pleasure in the activities. The question is whether we shall do so as men and women, or as beasts.

It may seem strange to say it, but to be temperate or moderate in one's desires for carnal pleasures is actually an aspect of moral idealism. It is a standard of excellence, and not everyone chooses to pursue it. We have all met hardened cynics like the cowboy in Tom T. Hall's 1975 hit "The Cowboy and the Poet," for whom the meaning of life was "faster horses, younger women, older whiskey, and more money." Down through the centuries, there have been many and seemingly reputable voices who have said similar things, such as the essayist Montaigne, who declared that "we must cling tooth and claw to the use of the pleasures of this life which the advancing years, one after another, rip from our grasp."[14] We have all heard one version or another of the siren song that tells us to become well adjusted by embracing our libido. The Christian tradition holds a very different, indeed the opposite, ideal, expressed here by St. Benedict, the father of Western monasticism, in the form of a rule for good works: "Deny yourself so as to follow Christ, discipline the body and do not be self-indulgent; put a high value on fasting."[15] It is because we wish to be free to follow Christ, because we wish to be in command of our desires and not commanded by them, that we should "put a high value on fasting." The baser desires must be tamed and ordered so that nobler desires may guide us — that is, we should think of self-restraint as a means of flourishing, a path to victory, a cherished ideal.

It was once the common ideal of our civilization. From of old, the wise have declared temperance to be the essential virtue of youth. Why? It would be unfair to expect the young to be exemplars of prudence and justice: they have not had enough experience or responsibility to gain those virtues. But young men and women can learn to discipline their appetites for bodily pleasures, and if they do not, we say that they are spoiled or ruined, or, at the very least, that their freedom to choose the good is threatened. It is Joseph refusing Potiphar's wife whom we admire and commend; it is David stealing Bathsheba whom we abhor. These

[14] Michel de Montaigne, "On Solitude" in *The Complete Essays*, trans. M. A. Screech (London: Penguin, 2003), 276.
[15] *The Rule of St. Benedict* 4, trans. Carolinne White (London: Penguin, 2008), 17.

appetites are unruly beasts that must be tamed if they are not to destroy us. If our heart is set on bodily pleasures, our soul will be imperiled because, as St. Francis de Sales noted, "whoever wins a man's heart has won the whole man."[16]

There are few things more unsettling than to find a mature man or woman incapable of restraining bodily desire. Think of the awful spectacle of Denethor gorging himself on his meal while the hobbit Pippin looked on in the film version of *The Return of the King*: it was a sure sign of his lack of self-control and a trustworthy window into a soul far removed from peace. It was also an artistic signal. If we see that Denethor cannot rule his own passions, we know that he is incapable of directing other persons to their good. Indeed, if we are to be free to serve others effectively, we must first be free from the tyranny of our lower selves. This victory is the first step toward interior peace, as spiritual masters throughout the ages have reminded us. "It is in resisting the passions, not subjecting oneself to them, that true peace of heart is to be found."[17]

As we are disgusted by brutish and degrading behavior, we are saddened when digital devices devour the attention of family members who no longer talk to each other, thanks to the pleasures of technological stimulation. There is a need to temper and restrain whatever becomes a powerful and disordered desire; if virtue traditionally starts with moderation of the animal drives for pleasures, today it seems we must also practice, at whatever stage in life, moderation of the powerful sensory pleasures of

---

[16] De Sales, *Introduction to the Devout Life*, 172.

[17] Thomas à Kempis, *The Imitation of Christ* I.6. All selections from *The Imitation of Christ*, a classic devotional work from the fifteenth century, are translated from the Latin text.

digital engagement. This can be as simple as fasting from our devices on certain days, at certain times of day, or during certain kinds of activities.

In media consumption, as in other things, fasting and discipline for set periods is not an excuse for immoderation at other times. St. Francis de Sales shows us the way forward: "Steady, moderate sobriety is preferable to periods of violent abstinence, interspersed with periods of great self-indulgence."[18] We must first make temperance our ideal, and then gently, forthrightly, honestly, marshal our daily lives behind its high standard. And we must do so without fear, knowing that the Lord of life, our Good Shepherd, will lend us his grace to protect us from temptations and, in time, to help us to bring order to our appetites, freedom to our actions, and peace to our souls.

We Should Set Our Desires on the Highest Goods

St. Augustine of Hippo (354–430)

There is a splendor in beautiful bodies, in gold and silver, and in all things. For the sense of touch, what is suitable to it affords great pleasure, and for each of the other senses there is a just adaptation of bodily things. Worldly honor, too, and the power to command and to rule over others have their own appeal, and from them issues greed for revenge. But even to gain all these objects, we must not depart from you, O Lord, or fall away from your law. This life which we live here has its own allurements, which come from its own particular mode of beauty

---

[18] De Sales, *Introduction to the Devout Life*, 174.

and its agreement with all these lower beauties. The friendship of men, bound together by a loving tie, is sweet because of the unity that it fashions among many souls. With regard to all these things, and others of like nature, sins are committed when, out of an immoderate liking for them, since they are the least goods, we desert the best and highest goods, which are you, O Lord our God, and your truth and your law. These lower goods have their delights, but none such as my God, who has made all things, for in him the just man finds delight, and he is the joy of the upright of heart.[19]

Questions for Reflection

- *Have I sufficiently purified my heart so that I esteem spiritual goods more than sensory ones?*

- *Do my habits of eating and drinking hinder me from accomplishing my duties by interfering with my sleep, by leaving me unfit for work the next day, or by otherwise endangering my health?*

- *Am I opening myself to temptations against temperance through insufficient vigilance in media consumption?*

[19] *The Confessions of Saint Augustine*, trans. John K. Ryan (Garden City, New York: Image Books, 1960), 70–71.

3

Steadfast

No one wins a victory without fight-
ing, nor finds rest without working.

—Thomas à Kempis, *The Imitation of Christ* III.19

The virtues that preserve our freedom as agents are twins: temperance and fortitude. By the former, we are unchained from
cruel shackles; by the latter, we are armed for battle.

We have been born into a life of struggle and cannot find
peace unless we first admit that we have been summoned to
toil and to labor, to fight and to protect. Long before the earth
took shape from the remains of exploded stars, the Evil One
set himself up against God and was thrown down from heaven
with multitudes of rebel angels. When Adam later fell, bitten
as Eve had been by the desire to rule himself without regard
to God's law, the earth fell with him, and so, beautiful and
orderly though it is, it bears its roses among thorns and offers
us sustenance grudgingly. Our pursuit of the good, then, takes
place in a context well beyond our choosing or our likes and
dislikes. We must strive to preserve life and to pursue holiness

in the face of countless and daunting obstacles, both material and spiritual.

"Fear is nothing but surrender of the helps that come from reason" (Wisd. 17:12). Fear is a terrible passion. Desire always has in it some promise of pleasure; it beckons, entices, beguiles. Fear appalls, unsettles, and puts us in a state of confusion. Great fears repel us. Without tremendous force of character, we simply run from them. Lesser fears shake us. If our firmness does not suffice, we lash out at them, often bringing more injury upon ourselves and others by our irrational self-defense than we would have suffered had we simply endured the pain, discomfort, inconvenience, or insult. Fortitude is reason's armor and the bulwark of interior peace. If our souls are steadfast, the many fears that must and will assault us every day will not conquer us but will stir us to effective service.

When Aristotle examined the virtue of fortitude, he took special pains to warn his students against dispositions that may look courageous but are not so in truth. One of these is the readiness to act impulsively that we see in the young or high-spirited person. Another is the willingness to fight or to labor under compulsion, as with the mercenary or the slave. By these facsimiles and substitutes for courage, we begin to appreciate the authentic virtue. Our fortitude must be interior, free, and rational. It is a firm disposition to overcome our fears for the sake of a noble end, for the sake of the goods that constitute the communities of which we are the parts, for the good of the family, the neighborhood, the parish, the business, the city. If fortitude is to be a virtue, it must be the result of our choices, our actions.

Yet if we are not ourselves soldiers, how shall we be trained in this virtue?

In the first place, it is by the consistent performance of our daily duties. Our Savior, the carpenter's son, taught us by his example not to disdain ordinary work, and the witness of the first Christians is unequivocally the same. Whether it is St. Paul stitching tents, St. Timothy attending to the reading and prayers, or Priscilla and Aquila, by their hospitality, making it possible for the Gospel to be shared, the early followers of Christ took up the task at hand forthrightly and with generous hearts. Scripture casts the exhortation to labor courageously in simple terms: "In all your work be industrious, and no sickness will overtake you" (Sir. 31:22). It is true that work is for the sake of leisure, and the highest use of leisure is contemplation and worship. We must indeed keep the right order of goods always in mind. Yet in doing so we must not forget that there are many people to whom we owe our productive work—of whatever kind it may be—and that if we embrace this work as service, it will strengthen our hearts.

The other universal path to fortitude is the daily exercise of ruling our own emotions and keeping them reined in by reason and grace. In his classic handbook for achieving interior peace, the monk Thomas à Kempis expressed the common Christian tradition on emotional self-command with concision and power:

> Put no trust in your present feelings, for they will soon change. While we live, we are most changeable, even if we wish not to be. Sometimes we find ourselves to be cheerful, at other times sad; now calm, then agitated; one day fervent, the next lukewarm; today zealous for labor, tomorrow lazy; sometimes grave, other times frivolous. You must rise above all this changeableness by being wise and firm in mind, not attending to how you feel nor how

the winds of instability blow you about, but with your mind entirely set upon the last end.[20]

This life of self-command is no trivial task. What foes are more bitter, more constant, and more difficult to vanquish than our fears and the irrational anger that can well up from our daily converse with others? "He who is slow to anger," said Solomon, "is better than the mighty" (Prov. 16:32). How very true, yet how difficult to attain the serenity that comes from fortitude. How are we to do it? By taking little steps of patience, perseverance, and constancy.

We can find valuable advice about how to live these aspects of fortitude in the letters of St. Francis de Sales. He wrote thousands of letters during his two decades as bishop of Geneva, some to religious sisters such as St. Jane de Chantal, others to priests and to men and women in the world. No matter his correspondent, he always spoke in the same voice: direct, unpretentious, and above all, warm. Again and again he counseled his friends to find their joy in spiritual things, to look to the saints for inspiration, to strive to maintain a loving attentiveness to God, and to keep in their minds concrete images of the Lord: Jesus kneeling in the Garden of Gethsemane, Jesus displaying his wounds, Jesus stretching out a helping hand, and, above all, Jesus hanging on the Cross. Throughout these letters, the virtues he most frequently turned to are perseverance, constancy, and patience. All three are dispositions to carry burdens well. Perseverance and constancy regard lengthy works, with perseverance being the disposition to endure the pain of the work itself, and constancy the determination to stick to the task in the face of

---

[20] Thomas à Kempis, *The Imitation of Christ* III.33.

temptations to abandon it in favor of other, more attractive ends. Patience is a more general virtue of suffering well, but it does have as its special task the bearing of pains caused by other persons. Patience, in particular, is a foundation for the life of virtue and devotion because it is a firm strength of mind in the face of annoyance and suffering. As St. Thomas Aquinas explained, patience "removes by the root the passions that are evoked by hardships and disturb the soul."[21]

As he taught his correspondents how to live these virtues, de Sales was always practical and encouraging. To a correspondent frustrated because her daily duties kept interrupting her intended scheme of devotions, de Sales wrote with gentle but firm words that adjusted her perspective: "God wants you to serve him as you are, and by the exercises and virtuous deeds that accord with your state in life. And in addition to persuading yourself of this truth, you must also make yourself to love your state in life and its duties, and to love them tenderly, for the sake of the One who has willed it thus."[22] To other friends, he sent similar counsel. Constancy requires "that our hearts [be] where our treasure is and that we should live in heaven." And while on this pilgrim journey, we must "walk firmly in the way in which the providence of God has placed [us], without looking either to the right or to the left." To walk in friendship with God is not the work of a day, but of a lifetime, which is why we must "begin again every day," remembering that "there is no better path to success in the spiritual life than always to begin again and never

[21] St. Thomas Aquinas, *Summa Theologiae* II-II, Q. 136, art. 2, ad. 2.
[22] St. Francis de Sales, *Roses among Thorns: Simple Advice for Renewing Your Spiritual Journey*, ed. and trans. Christopher O. Blum (Manchester, NH: Sophia Institute Press, 2014), 51–52.

to think that you have done enough." The great obstacle in this attempt is, of course, our own weakness. Yet perseverance itself requires that we have a certain disregard for our shortcomings and maintain our confidence in the Lord: "God will hold you in his hand," the saint wrote, "and if he lets you stumble, it will be only so that you realize that you would collapse entirely if he did not hold you, and thus to make you tighten your grip upon his hand."[23]

The appeal to the imagination was characteristic of de Sales's spirituality, and when attempting to shore up the patience of his friends, he typically asked them to bring to mind some moment in the life of Jesus. To a friend suffering from fear, he wrote: "Be firm in your resolutions. Stay in the boat. Let the storm come. While Jesus lives, you will not die." To one suffering from depression, he employed stronger medicine: "Continue to embrace our crucified Lord, and give him your heart and consecrate your mind to him with your affections just as they are." And to one who had complained of bitter suffering, he used the very strongest: "Every day you should bring to mind the sufferings our Lord endured for our redemption ... and consider how good it is for you to participate in them."[24] The image of the crucified Savior is the right medicine for our souls: "The whole life of Christ was a Cross and martyrdom, yet you seek rest and joy?"[25] We may be tempted to soothe psychological pain with the false relief of digital distraction, but this is cowardice, not courage, and cannot possibly heal us. When self-pity or stress, suffering, or boredom knocks at the door, we must turn to the Cross and look upon the

---

[23] Ibid., 73, 93, 60, 24.
[24] Ibid., 79, 63, 29.
[25] Thomas à Kempis, *The Imitation of Christ* II.12.

Lord. He can cast away the darkness of our sorrows and fears and renew our minds for the labors of the Christian life.

Soldiers of Christ

2 Timothy 2:1–7

You then, my son, be strong in the grace that is in Christ Jesus, and what you have heard from me before many witnesses entrust to faithful men who will be able to teach others also. Take your share of suffering as a good soldier of Christ Jesus. No soldier on service gets entangled in civilian pursuits, since his aim is to satisfy the one who enlisted him. An athlete is not crowned unless he competes according to the rules. It is the hard-working farmer who ought to have the first share of the crops. Think over what I say, for the Lord will grant you understanding in everything.

Questions for Reflection

- *Do I keep in mind the duties of my state in life, so that I may recognize the obstacles and suffering that confront me as opportunities to serve God's kingdom?*

- *Is there sufficient order in my daily life — my waking, sleeping, exercise, and fruitful use of time — so that I am ready to labor cheerfully and effectively in the service of others?*

- *Am I allowing myself to be susceptible to anxiety, fear, and irrational anger by failing to think about God's goodness and his providential care for me?*

4

Poor in Spirit

No one said that any of the things which he possessed was his own.

—Acts 4:32

If there is a virtue that we are prone to misunderstand today, it is the one known to the ancients as liberality and to the Christian tradition as detachment from material possessions. We know that the poor in spirit have been promised the kingdom of heaven, but do we expect any consolation from poverty here on earth? To Aristotle, the name of the virtue that governs the right use of money was a Greek word that meant freedom. The implication of the name was evident: the miser and the wastrel are both possessed by their possessions and their desire for more of them, but the man or woman with a rightly ordered passion for the things that money can buy is said to be free and the master or mistress of those possessions.

We may be inclined to doubt that we need such a virtue. Why, after all, would not the virtue of justice suffice to regulate our use of money and of the things that money can buy? If we are law-abiding, fulfill our contracts and the responsibilities of our employment, and seek profit only from economic activity that benefits the common good, what more is there to do or to be asked of us?

The answer, of course, is that there is work to be done within, in our desires, because unless we are interiorly free from the desire for wealth and for the trappings of wealth, we will fail to be at peace.

The witness of the Christian tradition speaks with one voice on this point. From our Lord himself there are many and stern sayings, culminating in a warning that strikes deep in the heart: "You cannot serve God and mammon" (Matt. 6:24; Luke 16:13). St. John the Apostle also framed the issue in terms of our heart, that is, of the deepest longing and commitment of our will. "Do not love the world or the things in the world," he wrote, "for all that is in the world, the lust of the flesh and the lust of the eyes and the pride of life, is not of the Father but is of the world" (1 John 2:15–16). Why do we need an additional virtue, one that rectifies our desire for beautiful, comfortable, up-to-date, and trendy things? Because a "greedy man's eye is not satisfied" (Sir. 14:9), and, as St. Francis de Sales unsparingly remarked, "no one is ever prepared to admit that he is greedy."[26]

Confronted with witnesses such as these, surely we can admit that we have work to do at the level of our desires. To take their measure is a straightforward matter; again, de Sales: "If you find your heart very desolated and afflicted at the loss of property, believe me, you love it too much."[27] It is detachment from our possessions, and nothing less, that is required for interior peace.

---

[26] See De Sales, *Introduction to the Devout Life*, 150. Partially adapted in view of the French original.
[27] Ibid., 152.

This detachment is difficult to achieve. Consider the testimony of St. Teresa of Avila, who wrote the following words to her brother, commenting upon a friend who had recently experienced a significant material loss:

> It distresses me terribly to see that he has not more courage for meeting this trial which God is giving him; for I cannot believe that it comes from elsewhere. Pray God that He will make him realize this, so that it may cease to upset him. That is the result of not being completely detached. Our greatest gain is to lose the wealth which is of such brief duration, and, by comparison with eternal things, of such little worth; yet we get upset about it and our gain turns into loss.... I was thinking today of how God bestows possessions as He wills, and how a man like this, who has been serving Him so truly for so many years, and has thought of his possessions as belonging less to himself than to the poor, should be so much afflicted at the loss of them. I thought to myself how little I should care if it had happened to me; and then I remembered how keenly I felt it at Seville when we found you were in danger of losing your own property. *The truth is, we never really know ourselves.* So the best thing must be to flee from all to the All; and it is well for those who cannot do so to meditate frequently upon this lest our nature make us slaves of base things.[28]

It is an astonishing admission from a woman advanced in prayer and holiness: she, too, felt in herself a disordered attachment to

---

[28] *The Letters of Saint Teresa of Jesus*, trans. E. Allison Peers, 2 vols. (Westminster, MD: Newman Press, 1950), I:333–34.

money and to the things that money can buy. If poverty of spirit was so hard for St. Teresa to attain, we must expect it to be a tall order for ourselves.

One of the first tasks for us in this regard is to admit that there is a difference between our wants and our needs. We must remember that the world has always been divided according to wealth. The poor will always be with us; it follows that we will always have to do with the rich as well. And the rich, that is, those who can afford to be tasteful, have an influence upon us entirely out of proportion to their number or intrinsic merit. Led on by our admiration for the fashionable, we can always justify the need for a better-made suit of clothes, a more reliable automobile, a home more suitable for the entertaining of guests and family, and the phone or computer with the latest security features and functionality. We must also admit that we face a constant barrage of marketing, the sole purpose of which is to root these desires as deeply within us as they can go.

If we allow our minds and hearts to be shaped by the things that the world offers us, one thing we surely will not gain is peace. That is a reward reserved to those who are content with simplicity.

Here again the wisdom of the Christian tradition is harmonious and clear. Right aspiration seeks only what is needful: "Give me neither poverty nor riches; feed me with the food that is needful to me" (Prov. 30:8). "The way to peace and true liberty" is always to choose "to have less rather than more."[29] Christ himself tells us to imitate the birds of the air and the lilies of the field, as well as the Son of Man who had "no place to lay his head" (Matt. 8:20; Luke 9:58). It is the kingdom of God that we must

[29] Thomas à Kempis, *The Imitation of Christ* III.23.

seek first, and with a love beside which all our desires for earthly goods must pale.

There is a deep reasonableness to this perspective, as the wise have always known. Even Aristotle held that virtuous people typically settle for less because they devote their money to noble ends, such as friendship and the common good, rather than to their personal adornment and ease. The late-antique Christian philosopher Boethius offered another layer of explanation. Our bodies are always subject to pains and threats, and we can always anticipate future wants, which is why we find it so hard to be satisfied with the material state in life in which we find ourselves and why we are so easily made anxious about our income and our possessions. The remedy, as he explained, is to keep in mind God's providential care for us. And one way that God cares for us is by lavishly giving us friends who come to our aid in time of need.

In addition to guarding carefully against our desire to acquire and to own, there are two other practical steps that St. Francis de Sales recommended for those who would gain poverty of spirit. The first is to "be often with the poor, being glad to see them in your own home and to visit with them in theirs."[30] It may help to remember, to that end, Mother Teresa's counsel that there are always those who are poor in some way or another—materially, spiritually, or emotionally—in our own families and neighborhoods, so that there can be no want of objects for our solicitude. The second is to rejoice on those occasions when we feel "the lack and want of some convenience."[31] It may seem a small thing—to offer up the fact that our clothes are not this year's fashion or that our phone is not the latest model—but these

---

[30] De Sales, *Introduction to the Devout Life*, 153.
[31] Ibid., 154–55.

small things, lovingly given to God, can remove the thorns of unregulated desire from our hearts. "Whatever we receive wholly from God's will," de Sales explained, "is always most agreeable to him, provided that we accept it with a sincere heart and out of love for his holy will. Where there is the least of our will, there is the most of God's."[32]

Godliness with Contentment

1 Timothy 6:6–12

There is great gain in godliness with contentment; for we brought nothing into the world, and we cannot take anything out of the world; but if we have food and clothing, with these we shall be content. But those who desire to be rich fall into temptation, into a snare, into many senseless and hurtful desires that plunge men into ruin and destruction. For the love of money is the root of all evils; it is through this craving that some have wandered away from the faith and pierced their hearts with many pangs. But as for you, man of God, shun all this; aim at righteousness, godliness, faith, love, steadfastness, gentleness. Fight the good fight of the faith.

Questions for Reflection

• *Do I have a steady habit of distinguishing between what I want and what I need?*

[32] Ibid., 156.

• Do I find myself wishing more for the things that money can buy—and that are relentlessly advertised in the media—than for friendship, a clear conscience, and the ability to know and do God's will?

• Does my family tithe and give to the poor in proportion to our means?

5

Reliable

A threefold cord is not quickly broken.

—Ecclesiastes 4:12

When we think of a person who would make a good friend, perhaps we think first of someone who makes us comfortable: someone funny, interesting, and accepting. Or perhaps the person who comes to mind is one who would benefit us somehow: someone generous, helpful, and kind. Humor, generosity, helpfulness, and so forth are all good qualities in a friend. Yet we all know people who have these qualities but are not, for all that, our friends. Someone could be funny but in a way that is insensitive. Someone can be kind but not ready to bear burdens or make sacrifices for others. Someone can be interesting but may not take an interest in us. A true friend does not merely have qualities of attractive sociability. A true friend is someone whom we can count on, who understands us, and who would reliably make an effort to help us.

Perhaps you are blessed to have just such a true friend in your life already, and so you have experienced what the joy of friendship is like. But true friends are rare. This chapter is not about how to find a true friend; such friends usually come into our lives as gifts of Divine Providence. Rather, it is about how we can be the sort of people capable of being true friends to others.

Healthy relationships are essential to achieving peace of mind. A reasonably stable and supportive social network can make it much easier to navigate the challenges of life. A fulfilling life is fulfilling partly through the emotional and material contributions of friends, family, coworkers, and neighbors. The quality of a friendship you enjoy is partly a function of your own potential for friendship, how worthy of friendship you are.

In a sense, every moral virtue is relevant to friendship. Virtue in general enables one for friendship. Aristotle, the first to treat the subject at length, said that only the virtuous could truly be friends. Think too of how the seven deadly sins — pride, envy, lust, greed, gluttony, wrath, and sloth — all damage the soul's capacity for social harmony: as causes of disorder in the soul, they impede ordered relationship. Thus, it is customary to depict Heaven as a true community, where virtuous souls are bound together by their virtue; by contrast, the suffering of Hell is, in no small part, the pain of social division and friendlessness.

In Dante's *Inferno*, the lowest levels of punishment are reserved for those who directly damage community by fraud and treachery of various kinds, including lying, flattery, treason, thievery, and political corruption. In Dante's view, what most damages the social order is the lack of integrity; it is falseness, deception, betrayal that makes great sinners fit to be devoured by the Father of Lies in a perverse communion of destruction. By contrast, as we know, there is no greater love than to lay down one's life for another (John 15:13), to be counted on even unto death. "There are friends who pretend to be friends, but there is a friend who sticks closer than a brother" (Prov. 18:24). Hence, the trait of true friendliness or sociability we focus on here is *reliability*.

Let your yes be yes, and your no be no. Lean on me. You can count on me. You have my confidence. I will stick with you. The language of friendship is the language of an encouraging reliability. In the limit case, the true friend is the one who will sacrifice everything, even his own life, for your sake. Yet even short of such an extraordinary proof of friendship, society could not work without the basic bonds of trust, steadfastness, and integrity. This is the case not only because coherent action requires a degree of predictability from others, but more deeply because for people really to connect with each other, they must do so through sharing ideas, convictions, and purposes. To share in this way exposes one to vulnerability, and so true sharing takes place only in a context of honesty and trust, without threat of abandonment or betrayal.

The basic activity of friendship and community is conversation. Healthy relationship makes possible genuine conversation, and genuine conversation builds and sustains healthy relationship. To engage in genuine conversation implies shared commitment about common ends, and, if not to pursue ultimate truth, at least to achieve mutual understanding on some matter or other. Without trust that another shares such a common end, true communication is impossible, and the exchange of verbal expressions can be only a form of manipulation, an attempt to exercise power. One of the most insidious social features of relativism is that it makes one feel trapped in a world where the only interaction is manipulative, exploitive; if there is no truth, then nobody can be trusted to care about you, your concerns, or your convictions except in order to take advantage of them for their own private purposes.

Besides talking, there are, of course, many other modes of communing or achieving social connection or intimacy: sharing gifts, speaking words of affection, offering acts of service. Yet even these are often described in terms of conversation: nonverbal communication, the languages of love. Prayer, even without words, is still conversation with God. Even the force of John Paul II's remarkable Theology of the Body is in its reminder that marital intimacy itself is a mode of holy communication, expressing profound spiritual truth with a physical grammar and syntax all its own.

If conversation is the essential act of friendship, a central requirement of friendship is standing by our words. We must say what we mean and mean what we say. This starts with being honest with ourselves: taking stock of our strengths and weaknesses, having a clear-eyed view of our history, especially our failures, but also our triumphs. A healthy examination of conscience and a good confession is an exercise in self-honesty and makes us more capable of being honest with and for others.

The virtue of conversation is not a readiness to speak unlimited or indiscriminate truth — as if reciting an encyclopedia would make one a person of conversational integrity. The virtue of conversation involves saying the right truths, in the right way, and in the right circumstances.

Conversation is two-sided and involves not only speaking but listening. Patience and empathy are essential to good conversation; we must suffer with another, seek to understand a perspective other than our own, even be vulnerable and humble enough to be truly challenged or corrected by others. Most of all, true conversation is work. It requires great effort to sustain, especially because the most important conversations cannot be planned, either in length or direction, but must be allowed to develop naturally. It requires us to filter out distractions, whether from the environment or from within the conversation itself, such as tangents and minor disagreements that are irrelevant to the main issue being addressed.

Again, the most important requirement of a conversation is the commitment to converse. We must genuinely desire to seek understanding with another, and we must have a character capable of pursuing that desire with sustained integrity.

Inhabitants of the modern world are constantly bombarded with messages. Marketing and advertising, even news media, are vying for attention by any means available. Out of self-preservation we learn to filter, discount, ignore, or deconstruct such messages. As a survival strategy in the age of information, this makes sense, but it can lead us to become cynical and not receptive to real communication. Another threat to authentic conversation is, ironically, our powerful technologies of information and communication. Digital devices can tempt us to think that the purpose of communication is merely to transmit information rather than to deepen a relationship.

One of the reasons we are drawn to texting and similar modes of communication is that they give us the feeling of control. We can quickly express what is wanted, without committing to the emotional work of true conversation. Consider how much investment it takes to make a simple phone call, by comparison with a text: a greeting, perhaps an apology for interruption, some polite small talk or acknowledgment of a previous conversation, listening carefully to the tone of voice to evaluate the interlocutor's mood and receptiveness to whatever you might want to discuss—all this before the substance of the phone conversation begins. Such work, such concentration of attention and emotional investment, we can avoid by sending a text or an e-mail. For some, that work does not feel like a burden, but one must be socialized into such work—as the evidence of today's phone-averse teens attests.

There are, of course, times and places where simply exchanging information is adequate. Perhaps it is unnecessary to call a friend to tell her you are running ten minutes late, if a text will do. On the other hand, sometimes a phone call might be better in such situations, and if you find that you almost always communicate by text, what might that imply about the quality of the relationship and your willingness to invest in it?

Parents have been noticing for some time a decline in basic communication, as have employers of younger people. This is not a technological failure, but a failure of socialization. Every new generation needs socialization about how to use technology prudently, including knowing when *not* to use it. It seems increasingly clear that modern information technology forms habits of conversing—and habits of thinking about what conversation is—that limit our capacities to be reliable partners in communication.

Previous chapters have treated basic ordering of the soul in terms of its appetites and desires. Temperance, fortitude, and liberality are basic virtues that create stability in the soul and prepare us for true peace. Yet it is not enough to be a solitary individual rightly disposed toward our desires and our goods. We are social animals, which means that we can be fulfilled only through right relationships with others and with God. The most basic trait of sociability—the capacity to be a friend to others—is the trait of reliability: to be genuinely available to and to trust others, including ultimately our Lord, who offers Himself for us.

The Joys of Friendship

St. Augustine

To talk and to laugh with them; to do friendly acts of service for one another; to read well-written books together; sometimes to tell jokes and sometimes to be serious; to disagree at times, but without hard feelings, just as a man does with himself; and to keep our many discussions pleasant by the very rarity of such differences; to teach things to the others and to learn from them; to long impatiently for those who were absent, and to receive with joy those joining us. These and similar expressions, proceeding from the hearts of those who loved and repaid their comrades' love, by way of countenance, tongue, eyes, and a thousand pleasing gestures, were like fuel to set our minds ablaze and to make but one out of many.[33]

Questions for Reflection

• *Do I give due attention to the people in my life, making extra effort for the people who most need my attention?*

• *Do I rely on easy modes of sharing information when it would be better to have a real conversation, either by live voice or face-to-face?*

• *Am I consistently exercising the basic traits of sociability — trustworthiness, friendliness, personal attention — that I value in others?*

[33] *Confessions of St. Augustine*, IV.8.

6

Noble

Have salt in yourselves, and be at peace with one another.

—Mark 9:50

✦

Important institutions and powerful people will often find conspicuous ways to display their significance: monumental architecture, grand gestures, elaborate ceremonies. This aspiration is natural and good. As human beings, we seek to order at least some of our efforts to high purposes and to embody that ordering in our physical trappings, our behavior, our clothing and architecture, even our diction and carriage. Think of the reassuring permanence suggested by Gothic arches or Greek pillars, the honor suggested by the elaborate rituals at a political inauguration or a wedding, or the solemnity of dignified posture and speech of a courtroom or a funeral.

If we are sometimes cynical about such pomp and circumstance, if we can find them pretentious, it is because we recognize that such displays can be hollow or inauthentic. Sometimes persons and institutions do not live up to the high ideals they display: we sense that the college is not really dedicated to the

A Mind at Peace

Latin motto inscribed high upon its facade, that the politician is not truly accepting a solemn responsibility before God, that the smooth-talking lawyer is obsequious and manipulative. The posture might be nothing more than posturing.

These exceptions only confirm the importance of authentic orientation to high ideals. Even the most secular lives seek occasions for displays of honor and grandeur. The instinct is healthy and essential to human life: if we cannot ever tell ourselves that something in our life is ordered to a larger purpose, how meaningless would everything else seem?

Our lives should be ordered to what is good. The observation is so commonplace that it can sound trite. In English, we compare good to great. In our practical lives, we can sometimes tell ourselves that we are basically good, as long as we have not done anything bad. Yet in what sense is good the ultimate end toward which we order our lives? That sense of good is exalted, grand, supreme. Our lives are not supposed to be merely good, as, for instance, four on a five-point scale. They are supposed to be off the charts, outstanding, excellent. We are called to be noble.

We can gain insight into noble action by reflecting on the basic experience of knowing that our work is part of something larger and more meaningful. Whether it is work in a family, or work in a modern place of employment, if it feels meaningful, it is because we find our purpose in subordination to a larger purpose shared by others. And we do not feel our work is meaningful if we fail to experience our efforts as part of a larger project shared with others: if we are an isolated and replaceable cog; if we do not feel trusted or respected; if, instead of feeling like a valued member of a community, we feel taken for granted by family members, exploited by coworkers, or neglected in an inhumane bureaucracy.

This is true even in the case of factory work. The innovation of the assembly line was a remarkable development of modern industrial work. Yet it was also experienced as alienating and dehumanizing. An assembly line can make the production of a complicated item more efficient, but the more complicated the product, the harder it is for any one person to understand his one discrete task as part of a more important whole. Assembly-line work — especially when it is measured and rewarded in terms of frequency of a simple repetitive action — is not rewarding because it is not experienced as sharing in a common project.

For the past several decades, some of the most important improvements in factory production have been attempts to restore a sense of common purpose to factory workers — for instance, by having workers act in teams responsible for more of the overall production. Each worker finds it easier to understand how individual tasks serve a larger project and has experience of the collaboration necessary to complete the job. Such an arrangement ennobles the work. Not surprisingly, management experts find that this kind of teamwork increases not only worker satisfaction, but quality and productivity as well.

If productivity management can see the value of common purpose for manufacturing, surely we can see the value of common purpose for a well-lived life. A noble life is lived for a high purpose. A common purpose does not belong to one individual alone, but is shared by many. Although the notion is often misunderstood, this is what is meant by the notion of the common good. In a subjectivist culture, where a shared conception of the purpose of life is harder to maintain, the idea of the common good easily deteriorates into a focus on public goods, that is, resources to be divided among individuals who each have equal status. The true common good, however, involves participation in a shared goal, in which the participants may have different roles to play if the shared goal is to be achieved together—for instance, as different members of a family, different positions in a business organization, and different members of a political community.

First, let us take a mundane example, easier to understand than a whole society but comparable to it: the Missouri Botanical Garden. This institution serves a variety of purposes, and these ends can be put into a rough order. The Garden has shops, restaurants, a press, and customers, so it needs first to fulfill its office as a business by maintaining the measure of profitability sufficient to sustain its operations. Then, like any other large corporation, it needs to provide a healthy environment within which its employees can develop their skills. All of this daily work, however, is for the sake of further ends, one of which is educational and scientific; the citizens of St. Louis are rightly proud of the reputation of their botanists. Nevertheless, those same citizens may also think that the Garden has another end, as a place to rest in the presence of the beauty and intelligibility of nature.

When we think through these goods, we see that they increase in their ability to be shared. The Garden's daily operations provide structure for the work of its employees, but their good chiefly extends to those who immediately partake of them: the customers and the workers who are enriched by their purchases and their labor. It is plain, however, that the work of the Garden is essentially pursued because of higher goods that can be more perfectly shared: the knowledge made available by the botanists and the refreshment of mind that visitors to the Garden gain by looking at its plants in their exquisite settings. The former is perfectly communicable. The universality of the Garden's mission—"to discover and share knowledge about plants and their environment in order to preserve and enrich life"—pays homage to the communicability of truth: it is not limited to members and visitors but extends to the whole world. In one sense, the truth about plants is the Garden's highest end, but that does not exhaust its mission.

Even though its ability to welcome visitors is limited, the Garden's statement of its rules and etiquette proves that it understands itself as providing an equally edifying experience to as many visitors as it can hold, and that note of equality helps to point us toward the virtue of justice. St. Thomas Aquinas said that "truly to love a city" is to "love its good in order that it may be preserved and defended," that is, extended over time to welcome new generations of citizens.[34] He would recognize in the smooth functioning of the Missouri Botanical Garden the fruit of an analogous love. In such healthy functioning, there is no room for disordered individualism. No employees or visitors may put themselves before the common goods that the Garden serves. Should a botanist falsify his data or a member dig up and spirit away a rare orchid, either would be excluded from the privilege of belonging to the institution. Such offenses would be regarded as threats to the integrity of the Garden's highest purposes. Within the community of the Missouri Botanical Garden, then, we can see that justice must be understood with a view to the common good of the Garden.

[34] St. Thomas Aquinas, *Disputed Question on Charity*, quoted in Charles de Koninck, *The Primacy of the Common Good against the Personalists*, in *The Writings of Charles de Koninck*, volume 2, ed. and trans. Ralph McInerny (Notre Dame, IN: University of Notre Dame Press, 2009), 79.

A Mind at Peace

Can this analysis be extended to a whole society? The challenges are obvious. A botanical garden is a voluntary institution, and we are not surprised to learn that membership entails duties and a code of behavior. In political society, citizens cannot easily opt out of membership, and so, as citizens, we are quick to protest encroachments on our liberty. Accordingly, some contend that we ought to think of justice only in terms of respecting the rights of others rather than as a disposition to pursue together a common good. Yet we do not have to accept this modern conception of rights as the final word. It is possible to speak of the flourishing or "common happiness" of a society. Like the flourishing of the Missouri Botanical Garden as a complex social project, the good of society must consist in the enjoyment of a peaceful and just order, a joint project that encourages and supports the citizenry in lives of moral virtue. Justice, as an overarching social virtue, involves all members of a community being ennobled by participating in the common good of the community.

In this light, we can offer a corrective to common misconceptions about the notion of social justice. In secular contexts, this phrase can only be about distribution of resources: justice as *the fair allocation of many goods to individuals*. This is what philosophers call distributive justice, and it is compatible with, and hence easily co-opted by, Marxist and other secular ideologies. We all deserve our fair share, but this is not the highest or most noble sense of justice, and it does not require a shared sense of noble purpose.

In classical and Christian contexts, social justice meant something more and higher: the ordering of a society for its healthy flourishing. Social justice, properly speaking, is *the full participation of many individuals in the realization of a shared goal*—what Aristotle called general or legal justice, implying ordering to a common end. Every citizen is ennobled by participating in a common, noble purpose. It is especially in this sense that justice encompasses all virtue: each part fulfilling its role in contributing to the whole.

The challenge of Christian life is to find nobility even in small things. We should not need trumpets sounding, red carpets under our feet, or laurels on our heads to remember our dignity and the higher purpose we are called to serve. Indeed, the outward trappings of nobility could distract and deceive us, making us forget the true source of our dignity and the true nobility of actions that serve a purpose higher than our own interest. A life of exemplary virtue is not made by large ceremonies and grandiosity, but by sustained attention to virtue even in small things. In this sense, even one of lowliest station can live a noble life.

As we have seen, to perform noble deeds, one must see his actions as ordered to a higher purpose or common good—ultimately, to *the* common good, which we may call simply *the will of God*. The truth that we are called, in every moment, to serve the will of God is reassuring in its simplicity and yet imposing in its difficulty. Why is this difficult? For one, of course, God is a great and mysterious sovereign, and we must be careful in claiming to know his will. The confidence that he has a will for us must be matched by a humility to take care in discerning it. One great aid in this is the reminder that his will for us is inseparable from his will for the whole human family—that what he demands of us is part of what he invites all human beings, our friends and relatives and neighbors as well as strangers and foreigners and people we have never met, to share in His great purpose for humanity.

Yet apart from this most basic moral challenge, the world is full of things that may shake our certainty that there is a will of God or a common purpose for humanity. Far from encouraging a unified view of reality, with goods ordered to a highest good, the modern world encourages fragmentation, disintegration, and compartmentalization. It offers us many competing goods that would bog us down in worldliness. It offers unlimited avenues of distraction, so that we seek immediate gratification instead of a steady orientation to long-term goals. It whispers ideologies and distorted philosophies that deny or disguise the idea of noble purpose, of shared goods, of divine life. In countless ways, explicitly and implicitly, in theory and in practice, the modern world calls into question the idea of noble purpose.

The antidote is to keep the will of God in mind. By offering our work as service to God, and by daily prayer to remind ourselves to keep our work oriented to God, we can help ourselves and others to bear in mind a higher purpose, to ennoble our actions, and to bring order and harmony and flourishing to our lives and the larger society. If great action is what we seek, it must start with interior order of heart and mind to God. Prayer is the key to justice and nobility.

Born for Glory

Saint Thérèse of Lisieux

When reading the accounts of the patriotic deeds of French heroines, especially the Venerable Joan of Arc, I had a great desire to imitate them; and it seemed I felt within me the same burning zeal with which they were animated, the same heavenly inspiration. Then I received the grace which I have always looked upon as one of the greatest in my life because at that age I wasn't receiving the lights I'm now receiving when I am flooded with

them. I considered that I was born for glory and when I searched
out the means of attaining it, God inspired in me the sentiments
I have just described. He made me understand my own glory
would not be evident to the eyes of mortals, that it would consist
in becoming a great saint! This desire could certainly appear dar-
ing if one were to consider how weak and imperfect I was, and
how, after seven years in the religious life, I still am weak and
imperfect. I always feel, however, the same bold confidence of
becoming a great saint because I don't count on my merits since
I have none, but I trust in Him who is Virtue and Holiness. God
alone, content with my weak efforts, will raise me to Himself
and make me a saint, clothing me in His infinite merits. I didn't
think then that one had to suffer very much to reach sanctity,
but God was not long in showing me that this was so.[35]

Questions for Reflection

• *Am I aware of how the different spheres of my life are organized and ordered to a highest good?*

• *Do I resent mundane tasks, or do I redeem them by keeping
in mind the higher purposes they serve?*

• *Do I pray to be reminded of my responsibilities to others, and
the orientation of my projects to the will of God?*

[35] Saint Thérèse of Lisieux, *Story of a Soul*, trans. John Clarke,
O.C.D. (Washington, DC: ICS Publications, 1996), 72.

Part II

Sensing Well

7

Resilient

Establish thou the work of our hands.

—Psalm 90:17

The great truth that body and soul are one has been solemnly affirmed through the ages—most recently in paragraph 365 of the *Catechism of the Catholic Church*—but we nevertheless find ways to put it out of our minds when it stands in the way of our desires. The first part of our journey was a reminder of this truth, through its proper effect: that the deeds we do in and with the body shape our souls deeply, cumulatively, and, in some cases, permanently. We are taking this journey because we wish to have more peaceful souls, and the first steps must be that we bring order to our external actions and to our desires as they relate to the things outside of us.

Now it is time to take the next step, and to address our souls directly, and to do so first by considering the senses, our soul's windows onto the world.

We begin with the most basic of them, the one we have in common with the oyster and the worm, the sense of touch. In an essay on touch written in 1950, the Belgian philosopher Charles De Koninck expressed his concern that "our culture seems to be altogether too visual."[36] Were he alive today, he could offer the observation without qualification. The digital media surrounding us and accompanying us from morning to night is essentially a visual phenomenon, however much it may also make use of sound. The battle for our attention is chiefly between competing sights, with sounds only occasionally vying for mastery; lowly touch is, by comparison, lost and forgotten.

An effort to recover the sense of touch must be a part of our strategy for coming to terms with the new media environment in which we live. Why? In the first place, as De Koninck pointed out, touch is the sense of certitude. It was by touching the risen Jesus that St. Thomas's doubt was healed, and it was the touch of the living Lord to which St. John testified in the opening line of his first epistle. We measure the reality of something, in the last analysis, by touching it, and that fundamental orientation extends to the way we commonly speak about understanding the meaning of abstract concepts by saying that we have a grasp or a handle on the idea. Secondly, and perhaps just as significantly, touch is the sense of the inside of our bodies. Aristotle was the first to make this observation, and he taught it to his students by asking them to make the experiment of touching something with their hand in a glove: the fact that they could still feel the object proved that the organ of touch was not the exterior surface of the skin, but something deeper within the body. When we ask someone, "How are you feeling?" we also testify to this truth: by

---

[36] Charles De Koninck, "*Sedeo ergo sum*: Considerations on the Touchstone of Certitude," *Laval théologique et philosophique* 6 (1950): 343.

touch we sense any number of the parts of our body from the inside out. Some of those parts, blessedly, are felt by only a few persons at extraordinary times; those who have learned of the existence of their kidneys through the affliction of a stone have experienced the sense of touch in a way that is entirely unenviable. From sinus infections to sore lower backs and feet tingling with the sensation we call being asleep, countless are the ways in which we feel the parts of our bodies. A lifetime of such experiences leaves no doubt that they are indeed *our* parts, and that each of us, although composed of parts, is one being. Few truths are as philosophically potent, or as necessary an antidote to the unreality of the virtual worlds we increasingly inhabit.

In addition to keeping our feet on the ground, the sense of touch is also bound to some of the deepest expressions of our humanity.

Touch is the sense of the artisan and of the athlete. A skill as simple as riding a bike makes demands upon our sense of balance, our ability to apply force with our legs and arms—rhythmically, consistently, and with bursts of exertion—as well as our feel for the handlebars. More complicated practices demand defter touching, as, for instance, the baker's sense of the appropriate moisture and consistency of her dough, or the firm hand at the tiller required of the sailor. To play most of our popular sports well, we must have a delicate touch with an implement of some kind, whether it be the reins of a horse or the handle of a golf club or a tennis racquet. And in the case of the fine arts, it is the ability to apply the finishing touch to a work that is the prerogative of the master. This tactile contact and experience of touch that we enjoy when making or playing or riding—or even driving—becomes a deeply personal part of our lives. Some of the most relaxed, joyous, and refreshing moments of our lives are when we are employing our sense of touch in these ways. And, for those who have pursued the art or game to a high level of excellence, the fineness or *finesse* of their sense of touch is proverbial.

For this reason, the sense of touch is our principal metaphor for understanding the virtue of prudence or practical wisdom. We speak of managers as being in touch with their people, and of especially capable administrators as being able to handle whatever comes their way. Sales executives, fund-raisers, and politicians must have a feel for their respective clients and audiences, and we say that theirs are high-touch lines of work. The sign of the practically wise person is that she can employ just the right touch at the right time to keep the common endeavor moving forward. Shakespeare has given us a memorable poetic instance of this ability in the prologue to the fourth act of *Henry V*, in which the king visits his weary and anxious soldiers in the hours before the battle of Agincourt, lifting their flagging spirits by "a little touch of Harry in the night."

The sense of touch is also one of the best servants of our growth in the knowledge of truth. Though we may find it hard to accept Aristotle's contention that the sharpest minds belong to those with the softest skin, we can perhaps appreciate some of the connections between touch and learning. Any serious student knows that the sense of touch—understood broadly—plays an essential role in study. "Seat of pants to seat of chair and pencil to paper," runs the old adage, and we can imagine Aristotle sagely nodding and reminding us that he was the one who said that "the possession of understanding and knowledge is produced by the soul's settling down out of the restlessness natural to it."[37]

[37] Aristotle, *Physics* 7.3.247b18–20, trans. R. P. Hardie and R. K. Gaye, in *The Complete Works of Aristotle: The Revised Oxford*

The famous ornithologist John James Audubon insisted that we come to know about birds not merely by seeing and hearing them, but by engaging our sense of touch with a pen in hand. "Note down all your observations," he said, and "with ink, not with black-lead pencil; and keep in mind that the more particulars you write at the time, the more you will afterwards recollect."[38] The same point has received a testimony almost startling in its clarity from Blessed John Henry Newman, one of the greatest minds of the last two centuries: "I think best when I write, I cannot in the same way think while I speak."[39] What exactly is the connection between touch and understanding? At the very least, the example of the craftsman suggests that there is a direct correlation between our care in manipulating a tool and the focus of our mind upon a complex task. The role of penmanship in classical education is not only about legibility for the reader, but about concentration and composure in the writer—and for the practiced penman, handwriting is relaxing and meditative.

As the value of a well-composed hand-inked letter suggests, touch is an essential sense in friendship. The firm handshake is the quintessentially American sign of equality, brotherhood, and common endeavor. The pat on the back, the arm around the shoulder, the affectionate hug: it is by touch that we mark the partings and reunions, the joys and sorrows of our lives. Touch is also, to be sure, the sense of the intimacy of married love, one

Translation, ed. Jonathan Barnes, 2 vols. (Princeton: Princeton University Press, 1984), I:414.

[38] John James Audubon, *Ornithological Biography* [1839] in *The Audubon Reader*, ed. Richard Rhodes (New York: Knopf, 2006), 608–609.

[39] Quoted in Ian Ker, *John Henry Newman: A Biography* (Oxford: Oxford University Press, 1988), 662.

of the blessings, as the *Rite of Matrimony* teaches, that was not washed away by the Flood.

Touch is the sense of healing and of charity. Like any doctor, Christ touched those he healed, while sinners and the sick alike flocked to him in order to touch him, so palpable was his power and goodness. Mother Teresa's charism was one of touching: she lifted, held, and caressed those dying on the streets of Calcutta, and they were consoled, even when they could not be healed of their diseases. Christ asks us to carry his Cross with him and to place his yoke upon our shoulders, and, through the centuries, the Christlike have always done just that for their brothers and sisters. The Hurons gave to their beloved missionary St. Jean de Brébeuf the name *Echon*, meaning "the one who carries the heavy load," because of his willingness to bear their burdens on his broad shoulders. The love of a mother is shown unmistakably through the sense of touch: holding a baby close to her bosom, picking up and comforting an injured child, assisting an aged parent who needs her support to walk.

Touch, finally, is the sense by which we most deeply suffer. Certainly any violent injury is felt, and, like the wounds inflicted upon Christ in his Passion, injuries from violence are the most distressing, humiliating, alienating, and traumatic that can be suffered. Such wounds can deform and afflict an entire life. Yet, thankfully, most of our bodily suffering is not violent: illness, the necessary accompaniment of the changes of the seasons, the changes in our bodies as we age, and the result of our labors. Solomon observed that our perishable bodies "weigh down the soul" (Wisd. 9:15), and we can surely validate that observation ourselves. The dull suffering of fatigue, chronic localized pain from years of repetitive stress, and the physical cost of effort: in so many ways, our work—whatever it may consist in—is known to us as laborious by the sense of touch. Honest reflection upon the human condition has always come to the same conclusion: our lot is one of toil, but the suffering occasioned by our labor ennobles us. The fourteenth-century poet William Langland expressed the point with a captivating image of our common humanity, which he presented as seen in a vision: "A fair field full of folk I found … of human beings of all sorts, the high and the low, working and wandering as the world requires … all for the love of our Lord lived hard lives, hoping thereafter to have Heaven's bliss."[40]

In our intensely visual world, we are newly endangered. If we retreat into the virtual realities disclosed by our screens, and handled at best by the swipe of a finger or the click of a button, we risk a grave narrowing of our sensory horizon. Not only will our backs stoop, our shoulders curve, and our brows furrow, but our hands will lose their suppleness, our arms their strength, our bodies the resilience we need to accomplish the necessary and the noble tasks of life. The remedy, then, is not merely to lessen the number of hours that we spend looking at our devices, but to regain those hours for the engagement of our sense of touch.

Bearing the Cross in our Work

St. John Paul II

Sweat and toil, which work necessarily involves in the present condition of the human race, present the Christian and everyone

---

[40] William Langland, *Piers Plowman*, prologue, lines 17–19, 26–27, trans. E. Talbot Donaldson, ed. Elizabeth Ann Robertson (New York: Norton, 2006), 3.

who is called to follow Christ with the possibility of sharing lovingly in the work that Christ came to do. This work of salvation came about through suffering and death on a Cross. By enduring the toil of work in union with Christ crucified for us, man in a way collaborates with the Son of God for the redemption of humanity. He shows himself a true disciple of Christ by carrying the cross in his turn every day in the activity that he is called upon to perform.[41]

Questions for Reflection

• *Have I allowed an artistic or athletic excellence from my childhood needlessly to slip away? Would I find a healthy and innocent joy in regaining it?*

• *Am I exerting myself sufficiently in the performance of my daily duties?*

• *Am I bearing the cross of my own physical suffering with patience? Am I helping anyone else to do the same?*

[41] St. John Paul II, *Laborem Exercens*, September 14, 1981, no. 27.

8

Attentive

Let the word of Christ dwell in you richly.

—Colossians 3:16

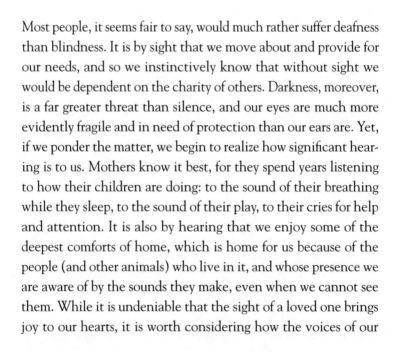

Most people, it seems fair to say, would much rather suffer deafness than blindness. It is by sight that we move about and provide for our needs, and so we instinctively know that without sight we would be dependent on the charity of others. Darkness, moreover, is a far greater threat than silence, and our eyes are much more evidently fragile and in need of protection than our ears are. Yet, if we ponder the matter, we begin to realize how significant hearing is to us. Mothers know it best, for they spend years listening to how their children are doing: to the sound of their breathing while they sleep, to the sound of their play, to their cries for help and attention. It is also by hearing that we enjoy some of the deepest comforts of home, which is home for us because of the people (and other animals) who live in it, and whose presence we are aware of by the sounds they make, even when we cannot see them. While it is undeniable that the sight of a loved one brings joy to our hearts, it is worth considering how the voices of our family members or closest friends stand out to us even amid the din of a crowded room. Faith, too, "comes from what is heard" (Rom. 10:17), certainly from the proclamation of the Gospel by preachers, but also in the stillness and silence of our hearts, where the Word of God is able to enter and to dwell.

As we continue our consideration of the senses and how they can support or undermine our peace of mind, it is well for us to admit that the exterior sense powers themselves are rarely the cause of our interior struggles; the real battleground lies more deeply within. This truth is especially striking with respect to hearing. Some people are, to be sure, hard of hearing or even deaf. Yet it is usually a simple matter for us to discern who in our company stands in need of slower, louder, and more distinct speech in order to hear us. It is also readily apparent, by contrast, who is simply not attending to what we are saying. Spiritual masters through the ages have written pointedly about our proclivity to ignore others, even God. St. Benedict, one of the greatest of those masters, so wished to underscore the critical importance of attending that the first word he wrote in his *Rule* was the admonition "Listen." By this word, he was not addressing so much the ears of his sons, as their minds. The ears, after all, do not have lids. While we are awake, they receive sounds. The question is whether we are listening.

As the distinction between hearing and listening implies, this sense is deeply connected to human experience. Human emotion is forcefully and subtly communicated through sound, as witnessed by the power of music to influence the soul. Even a visual medium such as film depends to a great extent on sound; the sound editing and musical soundtrack can make or break a movie. Sound is also inherently extended in the dimension of time. The eye can take in a vast scene almost at once, but one must have patience to receive the fullness of a song or of a speech.

Finally, the work of listening to human language is more than receiving a stimulus of signs, but requires us to marshal complex powers of emotional sensitivity, anticipation, and interpretation.

Today, it is better known than ever that the failure to attend is not always a defect of the will. Neuroscience and psychiatry have discovered that attention deficit disorder (ADD) is a malady of the brain, or, to use an older idiom, of the interior sense powers. These powers—exercised by our marvelous brain—were first discussed with precision by Aristotle in his work *On the Soul*. Almost two millennia later, St. Thomas Aquinas devoted considerable effort to understanding them. In this and the next four chapters, we will follow Aquinas's account and consider the work of the four interior senses. Today, through the use of brain scans, we can correlate their performance with the firing of neurons. Nevertheless, like the exterior senses, the interior can be understood only with reference to our awareness of those aspects of the world that they register for us, that is, the sensible qualities of material things.

Aristotle and Aquinas gave the first of these interior sense powers a name that is apt to cause us some confusion: they called it the common sense. What they intended to signify by that name has no relation whatsoever to the faculty of good judgment that comes to mind when we hear or use the phrase. Yet, as there is no ready alternative, we will continue to use it here, understanding it, as Aristotle did, as the interior root of our sensation where the sense impressions of the five exterior senses come together—thus the name "common"—and are sorted out from one another. How do we know that we have such a power as the common sense? Because we can distinguish colors, tastes, sounds, and the other sensible qualities from one another at the level of sense impressions. We do not have to learn from a book or by being told that the white we see is not the same as the sweet we taste; we are aware of the distinction before we have words to describe it. The common sense is also the power of sensory attention. Lying at the root of the five exterior senses, it is, in a way, the traffic cop of our sensory lives, waving some sensations along while holding others up. It is with a defect in this function of sorting and ordering sensations that those with attention deficit disorder must learn to cope. When we lack the ability to filter the data of our exterior senses, we are overwhelmed, less in control of our surroundings, and likely anxious. If you have ever been in a train station at rush hour or at Lowe's on a busy Saturday morning, you can perhaps begin to guess what kind of disorientation results from the common sense's inability to perform its function fully.

Today one often hears people say things such as "We all have ADD now," usually accompanied by a sheepish gesture toward their smartphones. A first point to make about such statements is that they would be less often made if it were more widely known just how deeply those with attention deficit disorder can suffer from their sensory difficulties. A second point follows from the first: if there is a partial truth in such statements, and if we are witnessing a change in our sensory lives caused by our habits of using digital technology, then it is imperative that we consider what is at stake.

Deformities and deficiencies of the exterior sense organs come from birth, injury, and aging, and so can deficiencies of the brain and thus the interior sense powers. Yet these powers also may be strengthened through proper use or weakened through abuse or neglect. The recent spate of books on neuroplasticity and the importance of training our brains is a chorus that confirms observations first made by Aristotle and Aquinas.[42] And because

---

[42] See, for instance, Aristotle, *Nicomachean Ethics* VII.3, and Aquinas, *Summa Theologiae*, I-II, Q. 53, art. 3.

our interior sense powers are the doors through which things in the world enter our souls and become objects of our thought and willing, their good or bad estate is of inestimable significance for our interior well-being.

One of the most striking meditations on the health of the interior sense powers is the tenth book of St. Augustine's *Confessions*. There Augustine considered each of his exterior senses through the lens of his habits of attending to them, that is, from the perspective that his exterior senses were under the command of an interior power capable of being either a good or a poor servant to his mind and heart. In an arresting confession to God, he related his past struggles with his habits of listening: "The delights of the ear had more firmly entangled and subdued me [than those of the sense of smell], but you broke them and set me free."[43] He chose to employ the language of slavery, captivity, emancipation, and redemption, and it is not hard to appreciate why. Many today listen to recorded music for multiple hours per day, and much of the time through earbuds that ensure they will hear that music and nothing else. Doubtless the vast majority of these habitual listeners would not describe their habit as a kind of slavery. The test of whether the habit has deepened to the point of becoming an addiction would come from seeing the result of their being deprived of it for a time. Even if the attachment to music were not to qualify as an addiction, it seems fair to surmise that listening, for many, has become habitual in the worst sense of that word, that is, only occasionally the object of deliberate and focused attention.

It has become a commonplace that our culture of constant digital connectivity is not merely different from its predecessor,

[43] St. Augustine, *Confessions* X.33.

but one in which it is more challenging to experience worthwhile attention, either in ourselves or from the people with whom we interact. Numerous commentators, drawing on research from neuroscience to sociology, from media studies to political theory, from psychology to literary studies, have described this phenomenon. Its practical manifestations are all-pervasive: there are new challenges in the pedagogy of primary education, in the socialization of teenagers, in the psychology of college students, in the communication dynamics of married couples, in the etiquette of a simple business meeting. For better or worse, we are undergoing a vast social experiment, and the early results are not promising.

What we badly need, if we are to navigate this new digital age is, in the first place, to incorporate periods of silence into our days so that we can appreciate listening again and begin to attend more powerfully to what we hear and to the people with whom we share our lives.

Should we succeed in cultivating a better habit of attending to what we hear, we have much to gain. From Sacred Scripture, we learn that the "mind of the intelligent man will ponder a parable, and an attentive ear is the wise man's desire" (Sir. 3:29). It is by hearing a helpful word of counsel or sympathy that our judgment is adjusted and our minds are restored to equilibrium and enabled to make progress toward wisdom. The Gospels are brimming with examples of fruitful silence. The first we are told of was the period of silence that the angel Gabriel imposed upon Zechariah as medicine for his incredulity: "And behold, you will be silent and unable to speak until the day that these things come to pass, because you did not believe my words, which will be fulfilled in their time" (Luke 1:20). The quality of Zechariah's subsequent reflection and meditation during the ensuing nine months can be readily appreciated from his magnificent canticle, the Benedictus (Luke 1:68–79), which is sung daily around the globe in the Church's morning prayer. Our Lord himself was not only often silent, but he taught the importance of silence as a precept, as St. Mark reports somewhat pointedly: "The apostles returned to Jesus, and told him all that they had done and taught. And he said to them, 'Come away by yourselves to a lonely place, and rest a while'" (Mark 6:30–31). Following in the Lord's steps, the wise through the ages have spoken with one voice: if we wish to cultivate a habit of good, attentive listening, the practice we must take up and make part of our daily routine is silence. The benefits are lasting, indeed everlasting.

For God alone my soul waits in silence,
for my hope is in him. (Ps. 62:5)

On the Good of Silence

Benedict XVI

Silence is an integral element of communication; in its absence, words rich in content cannot exist. In silence, we are better able to listen to and understand ourselves; ideas come to birth and acquire depth; we understand with greater clarity what it is we want to say and what we expect from others; and we choose how to express ourselves. By remaining silent we allow the other person to speak, to express him or herself; and we avoid being tied simply to our own words and ideas without them being adequately tested. In this way, space is created for mutual listening, and deeper human relationships become possible. It is often in silence, for example, that we observe the most authentic communication taking place between people who are in love: gestures, facial expressions, and body language are signs by which they reveal themselves to each other. Joy, anxiety, and suffering can all be communicated in silence — indeed it provides them with a particularly powerful mode of expression. Silence, then, gives rise to even more active communication, requiring sensitivity and a capacity to listen that often makes manifest the true measure and nature of the relationships involved. When messages and information are plentiful, silence becomes essential if we are to distinguish what is important from what is insignificant or secondary. Deeper reflection helps us to discover the links between events that at first sight seem unconnected, to make evaluations, to analyze messages; this makes it possible to share thoughtful and relevant opinions, giving rise to an authentic body of shared knowledge. For this to happen, it is necessary to develop an appropriate environment, a kind of 'eco-system' that maintains a just equilibrium between silence, words, images, and sounds.[44]

Questions for Reflection

• *Am I entangled by the pleasures of the ear? Do I find it difficult to work or to relax without music playing?*

• *Do I make a point of listening well to others? Would my friends and coworkers describe me as a good listener?*

• *Have I set aside sufficient time every day for silent contemplation?*

[44] Benedict XVI, "Silence and Word: Path of Evangelization," Message for the 46th World Communications Day, May 20, 2012.

9

Watchful

Take heed, watch; for you do not know when the time will come.

—Mark 13:33

In the beginning, God created light, and of all inanimate things, it remains the one most fascinating to us. It is by light that we see; the colors of the things that we see are borne to our eyes on beams of light that differ in wavelength and intensity. It is true that there are some creatures with much better eyesight than ours, and it is also true that we exceed the other creatures chiefly in the use of our hands, the tool of tools, by which we shape and form and bring to perfection all that we need for life. Nevertheless, we human beings are sight-dominant creatures. Just as dogs are led by their noses, so we are led by our eyes, sometimes to dreamy reverie, as we gaze at a lovely sunset or dawn, and sometimes to quick and alarmed reaction, as when our reflexes save us from impending disaster while driving. It is our sight dominance that makes the digital age at once so promising and so logical a development of human culture, and also so dangerous. We are apt to be drawn to the light of a screen, whether it be a television or a smartphone, and captivated by its colors. More dangerously—and perhaps diabolically—we are apt to be drawn into different worlds altogether, virtual worlds created by and in light. If we are to navigate this digital era, we must learn how to discern true from false seeing.

We come to the crossroads of our subject: the habit of using our sense of sight. We must now consider directly the most iconic artifact of the digital age: the smartphone. Portable, interactive, and infinite in its possibilities, the smartphone is said to have abolished boredom. Yet we must think about what a claim such as this might mean. It does not mean that the smartphone has given us a deep, meaningful sense of purpose and peace. It does not mean that the smartphone gives us mindfulness, meditation, or contemplation. It does not mean that the smartphone provides focus, insight, patience, and joy. It does not mean that the smartphone makes us watchful. Would Jesus have been pleased with the disciples if, instead of finding them asleep in the Garden of Gethsemane, he found them gazing into flickering screens? We can say that the smartphone has abolished boredom only in the sense that it gives a constant stream of stimulation. The smartphone is a distraction device.

It is also an addiction device. Empirical data in support of that conclusion are coming in fast and furious. Some of the data are just what we would expect: students performing poorly in their academic pursuits; youth spending more time on their smartphones each day than in any other activity—and sometimes more than all other activities put together; a chronic tendency of those surveyed to underreport their actual usage of the devices; and, for the leading brand, a 99 percent renewal rate, a level of commercial success hitherto unheard of and perhaps even undreamt of. Other signs are more alarming: drastic disturbances of sleep habits; the menace of Internet bullying and stalking; an increase in clinical anxiety; the scourge of pornography; a spate of suicides associated with the use of social media. Yet the studies and trends only confirm what we all know and feel to be true. Some two-thirds of adult Americans now use smartphones; we all possess sufficient anecdotal experience to persuade us that what the headlines suggest ought to be taken seriously.

The morbid subject of smartphone addiction must be squarely confronted, lest we mistakenly persuade ourselves that it is a passing phase.[45] Quite the contrary: smartphone addiction is the coming to fruition of well over fifty years of deepening addiction to the lights and colors of screens. Given our physiology, it is a development that makes sense. And for some, it makes lots and lots of dollars. It is possible today to invest in a company that researches and implements methods of inducing addiction to smartphone apps. What does it mean to be addicted to distractions? It will take the balance of this book to follow the ramifications of the malady, but, in short, it is the loss of the ability to have thoughts that are sufficiently deep and long to be adequate to our interior needs.

The phenomenon of addiction reminds us that habits are not always good habits. What is the difference between distraction and responsible attention, between mind-numbing watching and mindful seeing, between losing oneself in keeping up with the next thing, and finding oneself in sustained reflection? To answer that question, we need to reflect on the virtues and vices of attention. The power to notice or pay attention to the world is

---

[45] See Adam Alter, *Irresistible: The Rise of Addictive Technology and the Business of Keeping Us Hooked* (New York: Penguin Press, 2017).

one of our most basic powers, and, like every other power, it can be used well or poorly. As we have seen, attention is a cognitive power, but not purely an intellectual one: it is first located in the brain with the power Aristotle called the common sense. It is involved not only in theoretical reflection but in fact in all realms of human activity, including everyday, mundane tasks. Our attention is aroused by and oriented toward things, and it moves us to be disposed toward things positively or negatively. Human attention is as closely connected to our own subjective desiring of (or being averse to) objects as it is to apprehending the content of those objects themselves.

That is why we need a true ethic of attention, firmly grounded in the reality that our happiness is all bound up with the quality of the habits we acquire. When those habits make us truly happy, we call them virtues, and perhaps the best way to appreciate the approach we need to take to attention is to remind ourselves of Aristotle's definition of virtue, which the Church long ago made her own. The definition first tells us what kind of thing a virtue is in general, which is a habit of making deliberate choices. It then proceeds to tell us three things about those choices: that they lie in a mean relative to our condition, that a rational account of them can be given, and, finally, that the precise mean is to be found by the judgment of someone who is practically wise or prudent.[46]

---

[46] For a recent translation of Aristotle's definition, scrupulously faithful to the Greek and appropriately precise, see Aristotle, *Nicomachean Ethics* II.6.1106b35–1107a1, trans. C. D. C. Reeve (Indianapolis: Hackett, 2014): "Virtue is a deliberately choosing state, which is in a medial condition in relation to us, one defined by a reason and the one by which a practically wise person would define it."

We make so many choices during a given day that we are apt to think many of them to be merely routine, such as tying our shoes or brushing our teeth. We should, however, be grateful for the many years of good choices that buoy us up throughout the day, making it second nature to return a greeting with a smile or a favor with "thank you," to pay an honest price for what we purchase, and to put in an honest day's work for our employer. Like riding a bike or flying a kite, virtues have something in common with skills: to be able to exercise a virtue or a skill is a kind of freedom, an expansion of our sphere of activity, of confidence, and of joy. What makes virtues—the moral virtues, that is—different from skills is that they are not merely intellectual dispositions but are also perfections of our appetites. As we discussed in part 1, the desires of the temperate, courageous, generous person have been rectified by reason and stand ready to receive additional orders. To have gained a habit of choosing in accord with reason, then, is to be stable, steady, effective, indeed, peaceful.

Moral virtues lie in a mean because our appetites can either be too weak, too strong, or just right. The mean of moral virtue is relative to us, because our bodies differ and so do our appetites. For a slim, middle-aged man to eat a twenty-four-ounce steak at one sitting would almost surely be a sign of gluttony; not necessarily so for a linebacker in the NFL. To point out that difference is to show how the mean where virtue lies is intelligible; virtue charts out a course of action we can describe and understand. We can also defend it with reference to our own good, rightly conceived, and to the common good, and that is what is meant by saying that the mean of virtue is defined as the practically wise person would define it.

There are two reasons why the discussion of moral virtue had to precede our present topic, which is the virtue of attention:

first, because the virtue of attention is not often spoken of, and so, in order to be understood, it must be presented in terms of a general account of virtue that is familiar; second, because the virtue of attention—at least in our present cultural circumstances—seems to require that we have some measure of the moral virtues discussed in part 1. Without a rectified appetite for bodily pleasures, a lively desire to achieve arduous goods in face of threats of pain, a freedom from irrational attachment to possessions, trustworthiness in dealing with friends and associates, and a high ideal of noble purpose, the difficult task of bridling our unruly senses is not likely to be attempted, let alone pursued in view of its high and generous goal, which is, in the last analysis, the attainment of wisdom.

In treating our need to be resilient to physical pain and to have silence as a context for attentive hearing, we have laid a foundation of fruitful asceticism for our sensory lives. Now it is time to take a positive step by making a choice for a work of attention through the control or custody of our eyes, a work of watchfulness. There are two necessary starting points for that work. The first is to recognize that not every possible object of sight is equally worthy. The second is to be persuaded that the office of sight is not chiefly to serve our sensory delight, but to serve our good as creatures with intellect and will, creatures who know and love. Instead of allowing appearances to direct and control our desire to see, we must let rightly ordered desire direct our vision, so that objects may be to us like icons through which to discern hidden spiritual realities.

Let us ponder two examples from the saints that can prompt the reflection we need. The first is from the Little Flower, St. Thérèse of Lisieux, a young woman whose lyrical and childlike love for natural and innocent human beauty is well known. As

her conversion deepened, however, she began to love mortifications for Jesus' sake, including sensory mortifications such as
this one: "I was taken up, at this time, with a real attraction for
objects that were both very ugly and the least convenient. So it
was with joy that I saw myself deprived of a pretty *little jug* in our
cell and supplied with another large one, *all chipped*."[47] A second
example is from St. Teresa of Avila: "It happened to me that
one day entering the oratory I saw a statue they had borrowed
for a certain feast to be celebrated in the house. It represented a
much wounded Christ and was very devotional so that beholding it I was utterly distressed in seeing Him that way, for it well
represented what He suffered for us. I felt so keenly aware of how
poorly I thanked Him for those wounds that, it seems to me, my
heart broke."[48] These are valuable testimonies of watchful seeing.
These two deeply thoughtful women were both decisively moved
by seeing two very different sights, neither of them at all pleasant
to behold. These are, to be sure, extraordinary moments in the
interior journeys of great spiritual masters, and we may find it
difficult to relate to them. The principle that these acts of seeing
convey, however, is the essential one that the objects most worthy of our visual attention are those that draw us most powerfully
to God. These examples, then, may be just the encouragement
we need to lift our eyes from the merely attractive, fascinating,
or new, and to scan the horizon for a glimpse of Christ.

[47] St. Thérèse of Lisieux, *Story of a Soul*, 159. Emphasis in the
original.
[48] St. Teresa of Avila, *The Book of Her Life*, in *The Collected Works of
St. Teresa of Avila*, trans. Kieran Kavanaugh, O.C.D., and Otilio
Rodriquez, O.C.D. (Washington, DC: ICS Publications, 1987),
100–101.

A Mind at Peace

Watching

In the passage below, Blessed John Henry Newman speaks of interior watchfulness, a kind of attention analogous to the one that we have addressed in this chapter. The analysis he offers, however, can easily be extended to cover our sensory lives.

Let us then consider this most serious question, which concerns every one of us so nearly; what it is to watch for Christ?... I conceive it may be explained as follows: Do you know the feeling in matters of this life, of expecting a friend, expecting him to come, and he delays? Do you know what it is to be in unpleasant company, and to wish for the time to pass away, and the hour strike when you may be at liberty? Do you know what it is to be in anxiety lest something should happen which may happen or may not, or to be in suspense about some important event, which makes your heart beat when you are reminded of it, and of which you think the first thing in the morning? Do you know what it is to have a friend in a distant country, to expect news of him, and to wonder from day to day what he is now doing, and whether he is well? Do you know what it is so to live upon a person who is present with you, that your eyes follow his, that you read his soul, that you see all its changes in his countenance, that you anticipate his wishes, that you smile in his smile, and are sad in his sadness, and are downcast when he is vexed, and rejoice in his successes? To watch for Christ is a feeling such as all these; as far as feelings of this world are fit to shadow out those of another. He watches for Christ who has a sensitive, eager, apprehensive mind; who is awake, alive, quick-sighted, zealous in seeking and honoring Him; who looks out for Him in all that happens, and who would not be surprised, who would not be over-agitated or overwhelmed, if he found that He was coming at once.[49]

Questions for Reflection

• *Do I have a habit of compulsive looking: at social media, at my in-box, at screens in general?*

• *Is my daily looking at screens making me anxious, giving me headaches, or causing me to have difficulty sleeping?*

• *Do I have a positive habit of looking at beautiful and intelligible things not on screens that helps to make me calm, encourages reflection, and enables me to learn about the things I see?*

[49] John Henry Newman, "Watching," in *Parochial and Plain Sermons*, 8 vols. (London: Longmans, 1920), IV:320, 322–323.

10

Creative

If any bad thought comes to you, make the sign of the Cross . . .
and try to think of something else: if you do that, the thought will
actually be winning you merit, because you will be resisting it.

—St. Teresa of Avila, *Letters*, II:767

We live by stories, because each of us is living a story. We say
that we have come to know someone when she has told us her
story. Reunions with old friends or far-off family members are
occasions to fill in missing chapters from one another's stories.
We look on as our children, haltingly, begin to write on the pages
of their stories, and we cannot help but anticipate how they may
continue to write, and we hope and pray for happy endings. In
the quiet of our conscience and at prayer before God we think
upon and share with him our story. "There is for all mankind
one entrance into life, and a common departure" (Wisd. 7:6).
Our lives are middles that join beginnings to ends, and they do
not merely come in a length that can be cut up into segments;
each one is a single drama. Our lives are stories that can only
be told in terms that ultimately reduce to comedy or tragedy in

the classical sense of those terms, that is, as stories with endings that make them definitively either happy or not.

That our lives are irreducibly dramatic is a feature of existence we never have cause to doubt. The wildest flights of fancy and tales of technological eternities pale before the grim reality, expressed with stark finality by Shakespeare's King Lear, as he held the body of his beloved daughter Cordelia: "I know when one is dead and when one lives."[50] Perhaps it is in part due to our instinctual flight from death that we are so inclined to tell stories, and even to invent whole worlds in which frogs turn into princes and threats to happiness are chased away by fairy godmothers and wizards. Yet we also tell stories, like *King Lear*, that force us to stare death in the face and challenge us to come to terms with it, and, thereby, with the meaning of our existence. Stories have tremendous power to shape our minds, our characters. Where do they come from?

The imagination. This much, seemingly, we all know about our interior sense powers: we have a storehouse of past sense impressions upon which we can draw at will, to fashion what we wish, without regard to the limitations of nature. Green eggs and ham. Purple dinosaurs. The bloody battlefield of Agincourt. Frodo and Sam on the flanks of Mount Doom. So powerful is this faculty, so bewitching, seemingly endless in its potential to fascinate and boundless in its reach, that it tempts us to be content to enjoy it alone and to allow it to set the horizon for our lives. This is not merely a temptation for the young. The imagination has beguiled some who, it seems, should have known better. René Descartes may not enjoy a reputation for wisdom, but he

---

[50] Shakespeare, *King Lear* V.iii.262–263.

was certainly learned, is considered one of the greatest of philosophers, and is still the subject of much teaching, writing, and
arguing. The fact that he was overmastered by his imagination,
then, is an important cautionary tale. Not only were some of the
more notorious defects and contradictions of his philosophical
system the result of an overreliance on his own imagination,
but he also saw in our enjoyment of our emotions—spurred and
stimulated by our imagination—the "sweetest pleasures of this
life."[51] A century later, the Scottish philosopher David Hume
expressed Descartes's conviction more directly, seeing in a "delicate taste of wit or beauty" the "source of all the finest and most
innocent enjoyments of which human nature is susceptible."[52]
What the early-modern philosophers expressed as a thesis we are
living. Secular culture may almost be defined by its tendency to
privilege a certain kind of sensory experience over the joys of a
clear conscience, the satisfaction of a deed well done, and the
possession of the truth. Secular worship happens in art museums
and theaters where the religion of culture holds sway. We all but
worship the power of the imagination; instead of praying, we
look, we listen, and, retaining those impressions, we imagine.

The wise, who have often been storytellers, have warned that
the imagination is a power that must be kept carefully in check
and bridled by reason, by our hold upon reality. "Divinations
and omens and dreams are folly," we read in the book of Sirach,

[51] René Descartes, *The Passions of the Soul* IV.212, in *The Philosophical Writings of Descartes*, vol. I, trans. John Cottingham, Robert
Stoothoff, and Dugald Murdoch (Cambridge: Cambridge University Press, 1985), 404.

[52] David Hume, "The Standard of Taste," in Hume, *Selected Essays*, ed. Stephen Copley and Andrew Edgar (Oxford: Oxford
University Press, 1993), 143.

together with this stern command: "Unless they are sent from the Most High as a visitation, do not give your mind to them" (Sir. 34:5–6). Recalling the tendency of our imagination to be led astray by indigestion, the spiritual master Thomas à Kempis taught that we should not let ourselves be "troubled by strange fantasies that come from what we have eaten" but instead should "bravely keep to our purpose and make our way straight to God."[53] Our Lord himself seems to have had our unruly imagination at least partially in mind when he explained to his disciples why he was so earnest in setting aside the Pharisees' preoccupation with merely exterior cleanliness: "Do you not see that whatever goes into a man from outside cannot defile him?... For from within, out of the heart of man, come evil thoughts, fornication, theft, murder, adultery, coveting, wickedness, deceit, licentiousness, envy, slander, pride, foolishness" (Mark 7:18, 21–22). To be sure, these capital sins can come forth into the world only when there is a perversion of the will, but they get their start in the imagination, which is a veritable seat of temptation, and, if we consent to let it rule us, of sin.

The imagination is an extraordinary force both for evil and for good. The amazing characteristic of our brains as organs is that, although they cost us an inordinate amount of energy to use, we are hardly ever conscious of their work. We are keenly aware of our exterior senses, for each of their organs is exquisitely delicate and can be the site of terrible localized pain or, what is sometimes worse, a disgust that is so awful that it literally makes us wretched. We cannot see without light and something to look at; we cannot hear if a sound does not come to our ears. Yet we imagine even in our sleep, and we can call forth at whim

---

[53] Thomas à Kempis, *The Imitation of Christ* III.6.

composite images built up of past sense impressions. Our exterior senses, like our minds, are bound by truth, by reality. If we frame two contradictory propositions, one must be true and the other false. We either see the thing, or we do not. The imagination is, by contrast, without measure or tether.

Jane Austen's rich and disciplined mind enabled her to explore the power of imagination even of characters who were not otherwise entirely admirable. Picture a comfortable drawing room and a family enjoying a quiet evening together with a guest, who offers to entertain them by reading a few pages of Shakespeare.

> Crawford took the volume. "Let me have the pleasure of finishing that speech to your ladyship," said he. "I shall find it immediately." And by carefully giving way to the inclination of the leaves, he did find it, or within a page or two, quite near enough to satisfy Lady Bertram, who assured him, as soon as he mentioned the name of Cardinal Wolsey, that he had got the very speech.—Not a look, or an offer of help had Fanny given; not a syllable for or against. All her attention was for her work. She seemed determined to be interested by nothing else. But taste was too strong in her. She could not abstract her mind five minutes; she was forced to listen; his reading was capital, and her pleasure in good reading extreme. To *good* reading, however, she had long been used; her uncle read well—her cousins all—Edmund very well; but in Mr. Crawford's reading there was a variety of excellence beyond what she had ever met with. The King, the Queen, Buckingham, Wolsey, Cromwell, all were given in turn; for with the happiest knack, the happiest power

of jumping and guessing, he could always light, at will, on the best scene, or the best speeches of each; and whether it were dignity or pride, or tenderness or remorse, or whatever were to be expressed, he could do it with equal beauty.—It was truly dramatic.[54]

Those familiar with the story of *Mansfield Park* know how ambiguous was this exercise of Henry Crawford's imagination, for Austen presents Crawford as someone with a need to perform and to be admired that can be characterized only as vanity. Austen's portrayal of his performance, however, remains a valuable depiction of the imagination's office and power. In Crawford's reading, there was certainly skill on display, an intellectual excellence, but there was also undeniably an ability to summon forth from within the elements by which speech is made into music: rhythm, tone, and the dynamism of emphasis. The source of this ability is the imagination, where thousands upon thousands of past sense impressions lie ready to hand, as so much tinder for the fire of expression.

The danger of such a faculty is now plainer than ever. The virtual worlds summoned forth from the imagination of video game designers and shaped in part by the imaginations of the players themselves are nothing short of captivating. The tales of young men descending into a state worse than slavery by their addiction to these games are harrowing and multiplying daily.[55] The virtual worlds of social media sites are little better; the border between what is true and what is merely imagined in posts on social media sites is porous, to say the least.

[54] Jane Austen, *Mansfield Park* III.3, ed. James Kinsley (Oxford: Oxford University Press, 2003), 263–644.
[55] See, for instance, Alter, *Irresistible*, 60–66.

Creative

Yet the imagination was intended by God to be a source of good inspiration, a powerful cause of creativity, insight, and innovation. The role of the imagination in the production of great works of art hardly needs to be mentioned. Who has not been stirred in the depths and moved by a favorite painting, poem, symphony, or song? The imagination is also essential for the historian's work. The character of a person long dead is like an object we see in the distance: two-dimensional. The imagination must supply the needed depth. The imagination is the interior sense of the scientist who seeks to explain the hidden natures of things and their unseen structures and origins. And the imagination is, as we have seen, the wellspring of performance.

The person with a well-stocked and well-ordered imagination, whose creativity is disciplined by reason and rectified by moral virtue, is a tremendous gift to himself and the world. It is the imagination that enables us to perceive the circumstances of our actions in full, as we draw together those aspects of the setting of our choices that are not physically present before us yet shape our choices and partially determine the outcome of our actions. It is the imaginative parent who conjures up a fun birthday party for a child, the imaginative spouse who finds a new way to celebrate an anniversary with joy, the imaginative friend who helps someone perplexed to untie a troublesome relational knot, and the imaginative employee who suggests a solution to a crucial problem at work.

Each of us can offer the gift of a vibrant and well-disciplined imagination to others, if we will but stir ourselves to be more than mere passive consumers of sense impressions offered by the world and its screens. A constant diet of prepackaged sensory stimulation makes our imaginations both weak and liable to be manipulated by others. If we would be as creative as Dante or

A Mind at Peace

Raphael, or George Bailey in *It's A Wonderful Life*, we must take charge of our sensory lives and work to make our imaginations serve the higher powers of intellect and will.

⁂

On Interruptions to Prayer

St. Teresa of Avila

Take no notice of that feeling you get of wanting to leave off in the middle of your prayer, but praise the Lord for the desire you have to pray: that, you may be sure, comes from your will, which loves to be with God. It is just melancholy that oppresses you and gives you the feeling of constraint. Try occasionally, when you find yourself oppressed in that way, to go to some place where you can see the sky, and walk up and down a little: doing that will not interfere with your prayer, and we must treat this human frailty of ours in such a way that our nature is not subjected to undue constraint. We are seeking God all the time, and it is because of this that we go about in search of means to that end, and it is essential that the soul should be led gently.[56]

⁂

Questions for Reflection

+ *What stories do I tell? How can my storytelling become more rich, more virtuous, more holy?*

[56] Teresa of Avila to Don Teutonio de Braganza, in St. Teresa of Jesus, *Letters*, I:147–148.

Creative

- Have I allowed myself to settle for a constant diet of pre-packaged sensory stimuli, especially in the form of television and movies, instead of putting my imagination to work by reading a good book?

- Am I allowing myself to be discouraged when I am interiorly attacked by bad images? Am I resolute in dismissing them and in turning my mind back to what is real, true, and good?

11

Perceptive

Be transformed by the renewal of your mind.

—Romans 12:2

King David marveled that God had made man "little less than the angels" (Ps. 8:6, DR [RSV = Ps. 8:5]). Our minds should indeed make us stop short and wonder. Aquinas thought that the proof for the immortality of the soul turned ultimately on the fact that we are able to know—at least to some extent—the natures of all material things. Were he alive today, he would be thrilled by the advances of chemistry, physics, astronomy, and biology, and see in them so many confirmations of the truth that we do not accept limits on what we can know about the natural world. If it is out there, we intend to find it; if we are confronted with a puzzle, we are determined to solve it. Unlike the angels, however, we gain this knowledge at great cost, both in the individual labor of study and in the collective labor and expense of organized inquiry. For we come into the world knowing nothing and must gain by the use of our senses what knowledge we enjoy of the hidden causes of things.

A Mind at Peace

Our senses provide us with so many indications of what things are and what causes them to be. We may not wish to taste the flesh of robins, as Audubon did, but we are eager to follow his example in other ways: to listen to robins' songs and calls, to peer intently at their plumage, and to examine their bodies with great care, perhaps even to the point of smelling them, and to compare them with bluebirds, thrushes, and cardinals. Slowly but surely, we arrive at a knowledge, however partial, of what it is, and we begin to be able to name it: an animal, a bird, a songbird, and, at last, a robin. And when we have learned something about the nature of the things we see and hear, that knowledge in turn informs our subsequent sensory experiences, and we recognize *this* as an instance of *that kind* of thing; we see *this* robin, *that* robin, *the other* robin.

The interpenetration of our sensory and intellectual lives means that we are a good deal more complex than the angels, who know without the need to learn through the senses, and it also means that we are more complicated than the beasts, which sense, learn, remember, and act by instinct, but do not know. It is from the contrast between our knowing and the instinctual action of the higher animals that we can discern the third level of our interior sense lives, the cogitative or perceiving power. The power exists imperfectly in the higher animals, which recognize certain kinds of things as the due recipients of a behavioral response, as, for instance, the spaniel recognizes the rabbit as something to be chased and another dog as something to be barked at. The human cogitative or perceiving power involves not merely an instinctual behavior; it includes a judgment, that *this* individual is an instance of *that kind* of thing. An illuminating example of the work of the cogitative power is found in Genesis 2:23, when, having seen Eve for the first time, Adam remarked, "This at last is bone of my bones and flesh of my flesh." At the level of sense perception, Adam saw

Eve, an individual, but seeing her, he recognized her under the universal categories of living thing, rational animal, and mate.

Another way of appreciating the office of the cogitative power is from a close examination of our common experience of one another as acting persons. That inquiry allows us to divide the work of choosing and acting into its three component parts: the act of deliberation, the act of judgment, and, finally, the act of command. Each of these acts can be accomplished well or poorly, and they build on one another, so that command requires both judgment and deliberation, while deliberation does not necessitate judgment, nor judgment command. For it is evidently one thing to make a judgment about the moral quality of a prospective action, and another to do the deed. Again, it is one thing to think through a number of circumstances and possible consequences relevant to making a judgment, and another to take a stand on which course of action we judge to be correct.

From the differences we see in one another's choices and actions, we come to appreciate the role of the interior sense powers. We know that our senses are involved because our moral decisions concern particular objects of choice, which come to our attention by our sensing them. It is evident that some people are more resourceful than others in thinking through the ramifications of a decision that confronts them; such persons can call to mind more of the relevant circumstances and foresee more consequences than others. This ability flows from their well-functioning imagination, which enables them to call to mind images that shed light on the situation. Others are known to be trustworthy in their ability to size up the universal that is present in the particular, to perceive that this action is an instance of injustice, or that person is not reliable. This kind of judgment is the work of the cogitative power, our ability to perceive *this* as belonging to *that* kind of thing.

A Mind at Peace

The perception of the universal in the particular is essential to the work of practical reason. For something to be the possible object of our choice, it must in some way be an individual instance of some kind of thing: *this* path to take, *that* house to buy. If our ability to apprehend individual things under the appropriate universals has been distorted or undermined, then we are unable reliably to choose the good in those cases. Today, we see mounting evidence of just such unreliability. Sherry Turkle tells of people who have seemingly lost the ability to distinguish between a robot and a living being, but other kinds of failures are not hard to identify.[57] There is a growing culture of acting as though sexual differences were a matter of human choice rather than of nature; of treating pets as though they were human; and of harvesting cells, tissues, and organs from the very young, the very old, and the critically injured as though they were dead and not alive. In some of these cases, the cause of error is grave depravity of will and intellect; in others, it seems that the causes may better be identified as a kind of confusion about what things are, which manifests itself at the level of the particular judgment, and, accordingly, in a malfunction of the cogitative power.

How does this state of affairs come about? Vice is, to be sure, a major culprit. The minds of those whose sense appetites have hardened in intemperance become inaccurate, as though they were perpetually in the grip of one or another passion or always under the influence of alcohol or drugs. Yet, as we saw in the case of the imagination and the common sense, or power of attention, the interior sense powers can be harmed by abuse and neglect. When our attention and our imagination are regularly captivated by stimuli more powerful than they can filter, those powers become

[57] See Turkle, *Alone Together*, 23–147.

prey to manipulation by others. The same is true of the cogitative power. The composite images that result from the editing of photographs are one example of the substitution of ambiguity for clarity, but others include androgynous clothing styles, patterns of behavior that intentionally blur the distinction between male and female, and all manner of computer-generated images and animations that depart from natural models. When such imagery is out of the ordinary, as in the case of Medieval depictions of the unicorn or Renaissance images of Medusa's head, then they are recognized as fanciful. The danger today is that when our sensory lives are dominated by man-made imagery, we are at risk of losing the ability to distinguish between what is real and what is not.

Still more widespread than this kind of abuse, however, is simply the neglect of the cogitative power. When our daily lives unfold amid artifacts and our most common tasks involve the dragging of pointers and cursors across a screen, the result is that we are spending less time coming to know the natures of things through the repeated use of our senses. To take one example, notice how our awareness of our environment is shaped by trusting a GPS instead of taking time to study a map. Following the blue line on a screen, we can drive through terrain and fail to notice landmarks, read signs, or even really know where we are. More traditional map navigation sharpens attention, gives us a sense of place, and furnishes the imagination with an interior representation of our environment.

This and other examples show that choosing one behavior instead of another can lead to the atrophy of the cogitative power, as we become less perceptive. It would be difficult to contest the claim that today we are significantly less perceptive than in prior ages. For instance, let us recall the story of Susannah told in the book of Daniel. She was falsely accused of adultery by two wicked old men, whose perfidy was exposed by the prophet Daniel through a simple test: he asked each of them to name the kind of tree under which Susannah and her supposed lover were together. The first said, "Under a mastic tree," the second said, "Under an oak," and the discrepancy was enough to result in their conviction and sentencing to death (Dan. 13:52–62). We are likely to be brought up short by this narrative: how many of us could reliably distinguish between an oak and a mastic, that is, a sumac? Yet our ancestors in the ancient world were convinced that just such an ability to perceive was common to all. Today, we may find it easy to tell the difference between, say, a Jeep and a Prius, and so tell ourselves that we remain perceptive. Yet the differences in man-made artifacts are significantly easier to appreciate than the differences between natural things. For art declares itself—especially when the marketing and sales departments help to shape it—whereas nature loves to hide. For most of us, the honest self-assessment is that we have work to do in this area of our sensory lives. And if we lose the ability to perceive, our very language and environment lose meaning. What does it say about the world in which children are growing up when the *Oxford Junior Dictionary* edits out words such as "acorn" and "buttercup" to make room for "broadband" and "blog"?

How are we to regain what we have lost? We must first come to terms with the fact that our cognitive lives are meant for more than our gadgets and screens reveal. We were created by God to come to know something about the natures of the things he has created and, knowing them, to learn how to reason from those effects back to their cause, from the creation to the Creator. The benefits of a healthy interior sense life, accordingly, are very great. In our daily lives, we will make more trustworthy judgments and act more rationally, and in our wondering about the universe and what it contains, we will be the confident knowers that we would like to be.

On the Importance of Guarding Our Thoughts

Blessed John Henry Newman

Consider what must in all cases be the consequence of allowing evil thoughts to be present to us, though we do not actually admit them into our hearts. This, namely, we shall make ourselves familiar with them. Now our great security against sin lies in being shocked at it. Eve gazed and reflected when she should have fled. It is sometimes said, "Second thoughts are best": this is true in many cases; but there are times when it is very false, and when, on the contrary, first thoughts are best. For sin is like the serpent, which seduced our first parents. We know that some serpents have the power of what is called "fascinating." Their eye has the power of subduing—nay, in a strange way, of alluring—their victim, who is reduced to utter helplessness, cannot flee away, nay, rather is obliged to approach, and (as it were) deliver himself up to them; till in their own time they seize and devour him. What a dreadful figure this is of the power of sin and the devil over our hearts! At first our conscience tells us, in a plain straightforward way, what is right and what is wrong; but when we trifle with this warning, our reason becomes perverted, and comes in aid of our wishes, and deceives us to our ruin. Then we begin to find that there are arguments available in behalf of bad deeds, and we listen to these till we come to think them true; and then, if perchance better thoughts return, and we make some feeble effort to get at the truth really and sincerely, we find our minds by that time so bewildered that we do not know right from wrong. Thus, for instance, everyone is shocked at cursing and swearing when he first hears it; and at first he cannot help even showing that he is shocked; that is, he looks grave and downcast, and feels uncomfortable. But when he has once got accustomed to such profane talking, and been laughed out of his strictness, and has begun to think it manly, and has been persuaded to join in it, then he soon learns to defend it. He says he means no harm by it; that it does no one any harm; that it is only so many words, and that everybody uses them. Here is an instance in which disobedience to what we know to be right makes us blind.[58]

Questions for Reflection

• *Do I take my sensory life with adequate seriousness, in the full recognition that my mind and character depend on the integrity of my ability to recognize individual things for what they are?*

• *Am I fascinated or preoccupied with fantasy or virtual reality, or even styles and fads, to the exclusion of taking an interest in permanent and real things?*

• *Do I exercise my ability to perceive individual instances of the different kinds of things as, for instance, by taking notice of the birds and plants that I see around me every day?*

[58] John Henry Newman, "Curiosity a Temptation to Sin" in *Parochial and Plain Sermons*, VIII: 66–68.

12

Experienced

My son, keep my words.... Write them
on the tablet of your heart.

—Proverbs 7:1, 3

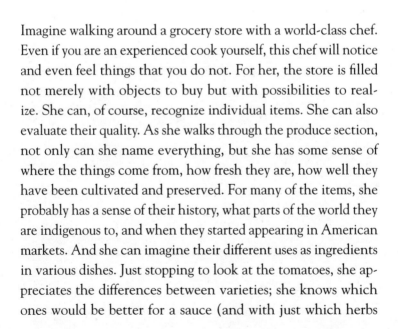

Imagine walking around a grocery store with a world-class chef. Even if you are an experienced cook yourself, this chef will notice and even feel things that you do not. For her, the store is filled not merely with objects to buy but with possibilities to realize. She can, of course, recognize individual items. She can also evaluate their quality. As she walks through the produce section, not only can she name everything, but she has some sense of where the things come from, how fresh they are, how well they have been cultivated and preserved. For many of the items, she probably has a sense of their history, what parts of the world they are indigenous to, and when they started appearing in American markets. And she can imagine their different uses as ingredients in various dishes. Just stopping to look at the tomatoes, she appreciates the differences between varieties; she knows which ones would be better for a sauce (and with just which herbs and spices), which might best be roasted or sautéed, which best sliced and served fresh with mozzarella, olive oil, and vinegar. As she walks around the store, she can envision several menus that could be created, taking advantage of the most interesting or high-quality items available. If she has a budget and an occasion, and the store is even moderately well stocked, the chef will soon be inspired by the world of possibilities before her.

Now imagine, by contrast, how the same grocery store is experienced by a child. Even if the child has uncommon patience and an adventuresome palette, the grocery store—and especially the produce section—would likely be experienced as an overwhelming confusion of objects. He would not recognize fennel, would not be drawn to the homely avocado, could not appreciate the dozens of possibilities latent in a single tomato. He could not recognize quality or freshness, or imagine combinations of ingredients that could produce a casserole or a soup, or how to bring out flavor with salt or lemon juice. The child would not see what the chef could see, and he certainly could not share the chef's inspiration. Most likely the child would be bored, confused, or overwhelmed. Given the freedom to conjure his own dinner here, the child would likely be frustrated and angry—or simply wander off in search of Oreos and Froot Loops.

These are two authentic encounters with the same environment. What makes the difference between the child's encounter and the master chef's? How can the child come to be a chef? It will not suffice to give the child a cookbook, or to show him some completed meals. It would be a better start to let the child help the chef in the kitchen. Yet even helping in the kitchen cannot substitute for what the chef has: years of training and practice, countless conversations with other chefs, the prolonged study and use of many cookbooks of different styles, and, of course, lots and lots of eating—thoughtfully and perceptively—her own and others' cooking. What separates the chef from the child, what gives the former a range of awareness and feeling that the child cannot even imagine, is experience.

Experience strengthens cognitive power. No matter how much we may try to pay attention, without experience we cannot see beyond the surface, make connections, or be aware of that which is not present but could be. Experience focuses and strengthens several levels of cognitive function, not only sight but also memory and imagination, and powers of analysis, comparison, and evaluation. The time, effort, and discipline of long experience may seem costly and limiting, but they are an investment in expanding the power to feel and to understand.

Because it extends our perception and appreciation, experience also extends our freedom. It is easy to see that the chef's experience, compared with the child's, is liberating. She is free to act in a way that the child is not. And what is true of the chef with respect to the grocery store is true of an experienced person in general with respect to life: the experienced person notices and appreciates more, and is empowered to act more boldly, more freely, than someone who is inexperienced.

One of the reasons our elders deserve to be honored is the simple fact that their long lives give them insight that can be gained in no other way. Where a child sees a collection of houses, his grandmother knows and feels the history of the neighborhood, each house with its own personality and story to tell, and those individual stories connecting her not only to other families but to the common history of her region and nation—its wars, economic crises, storms and droughts, sorrows and triumphs.

Perhaps much of this accumulated experience seems useless, and eliciting it seems nothing more than an exercise in nostalgia.

A Mind at Peace

One well-told story might help the child to gain new appreciation for some element of Grandma's life; but, alas, the child is likely to get bored if Grandma tells too many stories about what happened to the family next door. Nevertheless, accumulated experience, even on the level of observation and not yet rising to properly intellectual perception, is a kind of wisdom and, as such, is useful. A real-estate agent who knows the history and trends of the community will have an easier time finding customers and making sales than someone with all the technical skill to sell property but no awareness of the background and character of the place. Better still—more successful, more sustainable, and more virtuous—is the real-estate agent who loves and cares for the region he serves and does not see each property only as an opportunity to be exploited for pecuniary gain.

What is the interior seat of our experience of the world? The memory, our interior storehouse of things sensed and understood. With the memory, we come to the fourth and final of our interior sense powers. The memory stands to the cogitative or perceiving power as the imagination does to the common sense: both are faculties of retention. In the imagination, we store up colors, sounds, tastes, aromas, and tactile experiences. In the memory, we store up the things we have seen, heard, tasted, smelled, and touched: the location of the house we grew up in; the tune of our favorite piece of music; the names of the capitals of the fifty states. It is in our memory that we keep our experiences and bring them forth to shape our actions. It is the chef's powerful memory that enables her to connect the tomato she sees to the recipe she learned long ago so that dinner can be just what it ought to be.

Memory lies at the heart of education. Much of our learning has been not so much training in how to think as the enriching of our memory, through the experience of nature and travel, where possible, but especially through stories, poems, and songs. Much humanistic learning, especially literature and history, is about filling the memory, enabling the educated person to associate a new and present object with its past forms, with its future possibilities, and with literary references. It is memory formed by travel or study of architecture that makes it possible to appreciate the design choices of a new building; and it is literary and theological learning that prompts a person to consider that the role of a tree in a novel or a short story may be an allusion to the Garden of Eden, the burning bush, or the Cross.

Modern educational theories tend to denigrate memorization, or rote memorization, as it is often called. There is a place for rote memorization; for instance, for mastering the dates of major events in history in order to provide a framework within which lesser events can be properly arranged. Yet critics of rote memorization are correct to this extent: the faculty of memory is about much more than storing bits of information. An experienced person, with duly enriched memory, has become deeply acquainted with past persons and events, far-off places and monuments, words and ideas, meanings and formulations, both through practice and exposure, some of it disciplined and ordered, some of it haphazardly accumulated. Experience is a hard-earned familiarity with something, a familiarity that is the tuning of memory.

Classical thinkers took training in the art of memory with the utmost seriousness. They conceived of the memory as an interior space, filled with rooms that could be traveled through. An interior house like this could be a place to learn new things, by locating them in rooms or associating them with objects. While this technique could be used for rote memorization (say, listings of dates or numbers), it could also be used to order and organize ideas. By placing key observations or theses in different rooms, an orator could give a long, coherent speech by mentally walking around the rooms of his memory.

We sometimes think that memory takes effort to employ, but the fact is that we are memorizing all the time. The question is not whether we will remember things, but which things we will remember. Not to put too fine a point on it, but if you spend a lot of free time watching *The Office*, every new experience will remind you of some stupid joke by Michael Scott. If, however, you spend more free time meditating on the psalms, your mind will more easily connect its present experience with Divine Wisdom. This is why Plato placed so much emphasis on supervising the music and poems that young people would hear, because he knew that their minds, their affections, and their capacities for belief would be formed by whatever powerful stories took root in their memories.

The practical steps here are clear. We must beware of how we allow our memory to be formed and take responsibility for what we experience and how we experience it. We should consider what we already value in our memory—family history, songs, and favorite literature—and find ways to activate and renew those memories. We should labor to cultivate a healthy and rich memory. Perhaps we can learn more about our surroundings and appreciate its landscape and history; perhaps we can learn new stories about our ancestors and share them with our siblings or our children.

We can take positive steps to shape our memory. By reading, and by prayer, we activate old memories and form new ones. Studies show that our memory is more deeply impressed by reading physical books than by reading on a digital screen. Meditation on Scripture can be made easier by the simple choice to hold a physical Bible, which, as much as (or more than) any other book, can become like a trusted friend with longstanding use.

Some of our most treasured prayers are designed to draw on and to activate our memory. The great power of the Rosary is in linking simple, repeated prayers to a series of memorable events; even if our mind wanders in contemplating a mystery, it can wander within the remembered space of that mystery and help us to experience, internally, some new element of the joy, light, suffering, or glory of Christ. Mary can be our model for a healthy, well-tended, active, and powerful memory. May she who "kept all those things, pondering them in her heart" (Luke 2:19) inspire us to keep forever alive our memory of her Son and of his glorious victory over death and evil.

The Magnificat

Luke 1:46–55

My soul magnifies the Lord, and my spirit rejoices in
    God my Savior,
for he has regarded the low estate of his handmaiden.
For behold, henceforth all generations will call me
    blessed;
for he who is mighty has done great things for me, and
    holy is his name.
And his mercy is on those who fear him from generation
    to generation.
He has shown strength with his arm, he has scattered
the proud in the imagination of their hearts,

he has put down the mighty from their thrones, and
exalted those of low degree;
he has filled the hungry with good things, and the rich
he has sent empty away.
He has helped his servant Israel, in remembrance of his
mercy,
as he spoke to our fathers, to Abraham and to his posterity
forever.

Questions for Reflection

• *For what memories and for what excellences of experience am I most grateful?*

• *Have I sufficiently tended my memory, or have I allowed it to become an unweeded garden?*

• *When was the last time I committed to memory a psalm, a hymn, or a poem?*

Part III

Thinking Well

13

Purposeful

Pursue wisdom like a hunter.

—Sirach 14:22

If we are going to be purposeful in life, we must be purposeful in thought and action. Previous chapters have discussed purposeful exterior actions, relationships, and sensation. We are approaching the goal of this book, which is discipline of the mind itself. Before we get there, it is important to address something more general and presupposed by purposeful thought, and that is purposeful attention. The ninth chapter addressed attention in terms of watchfulness, especially custody of the eyes. Here we address attention more broadly as the overall direction of our whole consciousness.

We take attention so much for granted that very little is said or thought about it. We *use* our attention all the time, attending to many things, but rarely do we stop to think about the power of attention itself. Once we take notice of it, however, we can see how crucial it is to a healthy interior life, and how dangerous it is for us to allow our habits of attention to become misdirected.

A Mind at Peace

To have reached this point in our journey is to have drawn upon your resources of purposefulness in thought. You have made a commitment to a course of reading and reflection, and you have sustained that commitment through a dozen chapters. Yet chances are that along the way you have occasionally found yourself interrupted, bored, or tired. You have likely met with a kind of spiritual resistance, cognitive friction, or mental drag. And so, you should be able without difficulty to affirm an important starting point in the attempt to think clearly about attention: that it is not something that is easy to give. Indeed, we all must contend with relentless challenges to our attention, obstacles both exterior and interior. To gain a habit of purposeful attention is no mean achievement.

One of the most famously attentive characters from fiction is, of course, Sherlock Holmes. What likely first comes to mind when we hear his name is his famous power of deduction, together with the exclamation, "Elementary, my dear Watson!" Yet logical deduction, as he practiced it, is a modest skill compared with its foundation in his extraordinary capacity to notice. "Mr. Holmes, you are a wizard," said one of his more astonished clients. "You see everything." Holmes's response teaches us something about attention: "I see no more than you, but I have trained myself to notice what I see."[59]

Holmes is like a hunter of clues, and as the figure of the hunter suggests, his success required a great power of attention. We can all verify that we give attention by employing a faculty that is higher than and in command of our senses. Attention requires that our

---

[59] Sir Arthur Conan Doyle, "The Adventure of the Blanched Soldier," in *The Complete Sherlock Holmes* (Garden City, New York: Doubleday, 1930), 1000.

senses be focused and tuned, and that our interior sense powers effectively filter out some sense objects in order to give precedence to others. Yet true attention also sees beyond the surface, that is, beyond what the exterior senses provide, by making connections and noticing what is not present as much as what is. To notice the features of something involves a sustained effort. It is, if not properly contemplative, at least ruminative, and it gathers up several levels of cognitive function: to give or pay attention to a work of art, say, involves not only our eyes, memory, and intellect, but also our will. When we attend to something, we draw upon our powers of understanding, analysis, comparison, and evaluation.

For this reason, the common English phrase "to pay attention" is misleading. We do not trade or exchange our attention, we *give* it. As with most gifts, this means we give something of ourselves in the attention, and we find that what we give attention to gives something of itself back. It is also not merely an investment of our thoughts, but also of our emotions and most especially of our will. Attention is, accordingly, an investment of our very self. "Tell me what you admire," said the Dominican theologian Servais Pinckaers, "and I will tell who you are."[60] We are not giving our full attention to a well-crafted story if we are not moved by the sorrow of a tragic failure, or the joy of a heroic victory. Nor are we giving full attention to a person unless our empathy, respect, and charity are engaged. Our attention is, for all practical purposes, our identity.

Purposeful attention is a fundamental virtue by which our interior senses and intellect are directed by our will, by our ability to choose. The most common words we use to describe the

[60] Servais Pinckaers, O.P., *A l'école de l'admiration* (Paris: Éditions St. Paul, 2001), 5.

power of noticing or awareness of a person who has developed a habit of attending well are metaphors of extension and texture. Our attention, or the insight gained from it, can be deep, broad, penetrating, subtle, acute, or profound. We may sometimes speak of attention as a kind of focus, as though it were merely a matter of making sure the lenses of our exterior senses are in the proper order. Yet we know that attention is, in fact, more deeply personal than that. Attention involves an extension of the self into the world, so that the world is more powerfully received into the self. It is the essential and necessary means of our growth in knowledge and of any progress that we make on the path toward wisdom. Attention shapes what we know and value, and therefore determines who we are and can become.

For this reason, the Christian tradition, at least since St. Augustine, has spoken of virtuous attention under the name *studiositas*. To our ears, studiousness may seem to name a merely academic diligence. To St. Thomas Aquinas, however, it implied any "keen application of the mind" whatsoever, and, as a virtue, studiousness was the right ordering of our desire to know.[61]

Whereas a properly intellectual virtue, such as prudence, is a matter of right estimation and sound deliberation, studiousness, or the virtue of attention, is a habit of inclining our awareness in the right way and to the right things. To have this virtue means that our interest in things, our desire for knowledge, is rightly ordered and deployed. It has the appropriate intensity, being neither too strong nor too weak. It seems to involve a kind of steadfastness or courage, capable of overcoming obstacles (such as bodily weariness) that frustrate it. Most essentially, however, it is restrained or regulated or moderated so that it seeks

---

[61] St. Thomas Aquinas, *Summa Theologiae*, II-II, Q. 166.

appropriate awareness or knowledge in appropriate ways. The virtue of studiousness is temperance extended to cognitive desire.

We can appreciate the work of this virtue by considering what happens when we lack it. Aquinas addressed poorly ordered cognitive desire or intemperate attention, calling it the vice of *curiositas*, which we might translate as "curiosity," except for the often benign or even positive connotation of that word as used today. Consider how knowledge, especially knowledge gained by the sense of sight, can fail to be directed at what is beneficial, through laziness or lack of discipline. Consider how our attention can be directed at what is trivial or meaningless, or even worse, at what is harmful, as prurient interest that leads to lust, or as vain inquiry that leads to gossip. Consider how our attention can seek inordinate pleasure, or even seek a kind of pain by indulging in the thrill of shock or horror or ugliness.

The curious mind wanders. Wandering can seem harmless, or even a form of enriching leisure, as when you browse the shelves of a well-stocked bookstore. Yet when it involves straying from one's duties or from the true path, wandering leads us into trouble. That is why Dante condemned Odysseus the wanderer to Hell in the *Inferno*. Experience proves that a wandering attention is not harmless. Consider how, instead of attending to other people's actions for their good, or for our own good, to seek personal encouragement or offer friendly counsel, we can seek knowledge of others out of vanity, envy, spitefulness, or pride.

The identification of *curiositas* as a vice goes far back in the spiritual tradition. St. Augustine accused himself of *curiositas* in book 10 of his *Confessions*. St. Bernard of Clairvaux called it the first of twelve steps up the mountain of pride. The origin of this line of thinking may be Evagrius Ponticus, a fourth-century monk, who did not use the term *curiositas* but was deeply concerned about the problem of distraction or restlessness. Even, or perhaps especially, for a monk, temptations to distraction were bitter. Evagrius was troubled by how the mind, which should be meditating on one Scripture verse, might wander to another verse. Or, what he thought worse, the monk who should be concentrating on prayer might feel restless and procrastinate by performing a corporal work of mercy!

Challenges for people in the world are much different from those of a monk, and the opportunities for distraction in the modern world are practically limitless, leading us much further astray from the duties of Christian life. Devices of digital connectivity are designed to enable our attention effortlessly to wander to the next thing. We hardly have time to mistrust a distracting thought before we have typed it into a Google search or checked a status update. And we tell ourselves that we are not wasting time, either because we think we are learning something or because we are so quick in our constant consumption of the latest news, video, or post that we fail to notice that we have left one page for the next.

Our mind loves to attend to anything, just as our tongue loves to taste, but so much of what we attend to is like tasting the chemically calibrated potato chip: a dose of empty pleasure that keeps us coming back for more, until, unable to stop, we have filled ourselves with empty calories. Digital distraction is addictive, and addiction is not a metaphor here: there is evidence that this is addiction in every behavioral and neurological sense of the term, and there are plenty of stories of people who, like the blogger Andrew Sullivan, felt themselves self-destructing from it and checked themselves into detox.

The simple solution is to limit your exposure to digital distraction. Instead of attending to images and information, attend to your physical environment. Attend to nature. Most of all, attend to persons. Sherry Turkle's extensive research has confirmed what we should all know anyway: people young and old are hungry for attention from other people, and the great catastrophe of the age of digital connectivity is that we are losing our sense of being present to others, to empathize with them, to listen and share a world, even to focus enough for that most basic human activity, having a conversation.[62]

There is much at stake here. Purposefulness in our attention is intimately linked to a sense of purposefulness in our lives. Evagrius rooted the sin of distraction in a capital vice, acedia, the fundamental failure of agency that we discussed at the outset of our journey. *Acedia* is usually translated as "sloth," which only implies laziness or sluggishness, but the spiritual vice is much more than that. The primary emphasis of acedia is on a sadness that borders on despair. Aquinas, following St. John Damascene, called it an "oppressive sorrow" that weighs on the mind and removes the desire to act.[63] As a spiritual lethargy, its failure is more in inclination than in apprehension, more in heart than in head. At its worst, acedia manifests itself as a discomfort with and revulsion toward goodness itself, understood as that which is supposed to draw the agent to act.

The opposite of acedia is not activity for its own sake, but purposeful activity. Mere busyness will not suffice; indeed, that is merely another form of acedia. Aquinas says that the failure to rest on the Sabbath is an example of acedia. Restlessness,

---

[62] See Sherry Turkle, *Reclaiming Conversation: The Power of Talk in a Digital Age* (New York: Penguin Press, 2015).

[63] St. Thomas Aquinas, *Summa Theologiae*, IIa-IIae, Q. 35, art. 1, citing Damascene's *De Fide Orthodoxa* ii.14.

wandering or distraction, ongoing or compulsive activity without ultimate purpose: these are all manifestations of acedia. Whether you procrastinate by lying on the couch doing nothing or by finding other projects to occupy you, you are suffering from acedia. The falsehood acedia tells us is its implicit denial that we are capable of purposeful agency. Whether through an anxious busyness, or a lonely and despairing torpor, acedia is a blindness to or even disgust with the soul's motive power.

Like Evagrius, Aquinas declared that acedia was the cause of *curiositas*. The digital age, however, with its temptations to *curiositas* unimaginable by Evagrius or Aquinas, has taught us that it also works in the other direction: *curiositas* can cause acedia. Without identifying sin with a medical condition, we can notice also that in clinical terms, one of the documented effects of digital addiction is depression.

So, the most basic steps we can take to avoid *curiositas* are those that counter acedia: get out and do something. But we should do so with purpose, and in a way that fulfills our genuine responsibilities. We do not want to be busy for the sake of procrastinating. We can fulfill a long put-off responsibility, or take up a project or a craft. We might dedicate some time to attending to our family members or close friends in conversation, or embark on a serious course of reading in the Gospels or St. Paul's epistles. Above all, we should strive to hone our habit of attention in prayer. To gain a deeper, more consistent, more powerful habit of attention will not be easy: there is nothing to it other than to bend the unruly will to the task. To gain an effective, focused attention is today a heroic accomplishment, one that, like any other virtue, can be won only through determined effort and sustained practice.

Purposeful

A Prayer of Attention

Psalm 123:1–3

To thee I lift up my eyes, O thou who art enthroned in
    the heavens!
Behold, as the eyes of servants look to the hand of their
    master,
as the eyes of a maid to the hand of her mistress,
so our eyes look to the LORD our God, till he have
    mercy upon us.
Have mercy upon us, O LORD, have mercy upon us.

Questions for Reflection

• *How long can I read or listen at a stretch without becoming
distracted? Am I satisfied with that performance?*

• *What skills, practices, subjects of study, or persons have I
neglected to attend to in recent years? What concrete steps
can I take to ameliorate those patterns of behavior?*

• *Have I made a concrete, sustainable plan for the pursuit of
wisdom, to the "renewal of the mind" (see Rom. 12:2), by
putting on "the mind of Christ" (1 Cor. 2:16)?*

14

Truthful

Let your "yes" be yes and your "no" be no.

—Matthew 5:37

Taken broadly, every part of this book thus far has been about the mind and its different ways of attending in our actions and in our sensations. In a narrower sense, however, we have yet to address the mind itself. We have been using it every step of the way, but the intellect has not been the direct topic of conversation. It is now time to turn our attention to our thoughts.

Human intelligence is mysterious and wondrous. In a general way, we all accept the claim that rationality is what distinguishes us from the other animals. From the earliest days of philosophical reflection, those who have attempted to speak about this distinctively human trait have thought it something otherworldly, a spark of the divine in us, our share of the transcendent or spiritual power of an invisible realm.

There are, of course, many ways to notice that we are set apart from the other animals. Man has been called the tool maker, the language user, the culture builder. All are true descriptions of our behavior, but they point back to a power more deeply rooted in us, our ability to understand the world—as well as things beyond the world—in a way that other animals do not. Some insist that this human difference is but a matter of degree, not of kind. Other animals use tools, communicate, and live together in organized groups. Dolphins vocalize to coordinate a fishing expedition; bowerbirds construct elaborate courtship nests; bees live in a strictly ordered social arrangement. We are amazed by these feats of nature, and they give us a sense of closeness to these creatures. Nevertheless, all this behavior can be explained by appetite, imagination, and instinct. There is no need to reach beyond highly refined and specialized sensory powers to posit a mysterious rationality beyond them.

In all the rest of the animal kingdom, there is nothing approaching such distinctively human activities as the fine arts, scientific and philosophical inquiry, or religious worship. Gorillas have learned to use signs, but in no way have they been able to create whole languages, much less read or write books. Among the beasts there is nothing like the study of architecture, which is not merely the ability to build but a kind of theorizing about building, nor the slightest interaction that resembles our political arguments, which are much more contests of ideas than they are mere battles of will.

The glory of the rational intellect is its ability to work with more than what the senses provide, to transcend the particularities of time and space and to apprehend eternal principles and immutable objects. Animals see and deal with the concrete things in front of them; human beings do the same, but in and through them we also grasp realities that do not and cannot have any presence to the senses: mathematical concepts, scientific theories, logical arguments, and the countless conceptual realities by which we categorize and understand the features of the world that we can and do sense. We are aware not only of what is here, or how to get what we want. With the rational intellect, we have access to what is true, and what is good.

The classical philosophical tradition accounts for this ability by noting the difference between what is particular and what is universal. The senses, exterior and interior, deal in particulars. Look at a dog; it has this shape and that color. Close your eyes and picture a dog; it will be one breed and not another, either a puppy or an adult. Our minds are not so limited. We can think and speak about the characteristics of all dogs in general without regard to this dog or that one because we can think about the universal nature of dogs, the common canine way of being that all dogs share. This universal nature has intelligible content — it includes being a mammal, and a mammal distinct from other mammals, such as cats and cows — but that intelligible content has no particular shape or size or breed. Indeed, it is only because it has no shape or size or breed that it can be the universal canine nature, common to every dog.

Our ability to live in the realm of universals is mysterious, as witness the fact that attempts to account for it trade in seemingly contradictory metaphors. On the one hand, it seems as though the mind receives an inspiration or illumination from a higher power. Just as the eye can see the visible object only if some light is shining on it, so also it seems our mind can grasp realities only so long as some kind of intelligible light is shone upon them. This was Plato's favored metaphor for the work of the intellect: by illumination, the mind is enabled to see the otherworldly forms in which the things of this world participate and from which they take their being.

A Mind at Peace

On the other hand, the work of the intellect has also been famously characterized as a kind of apprehension, that is, quite literally, a grasping. It is as if the mind can take an image presented to it by the imagination, and by its own activity retrieve from that image some general, transferable intelligible content. This was Aristotle's favored metaphor for the work of intellect: by abstraction—literally, drawing forth—the mind can isolate and grasp the hidden forms that are obscured in and intertwined with the material things that they structure.

Aquinas did not think it necessary to choose between these metaphors. As metaphors, they each capture some crucial aspect of our intellectual power, and both shed some light on the indubitable fact that we can and do know. The point of both metaphors is that there are realities—truths, forms, ideas, universal structures—unavailable to the lesser beasts but made present to us in and through the mind's distinctive power. The sign of that knowing is that we can navigate the world of things, naming them, saying something about their properties, and comparing them with one another in an ordered way. This is a dog; that is a cat. Both of these are mammals, vertebrates, animals.

The ancients thought that mathematics was especially noble for giving us access to universals that go beyond what the senses supply. There are, to be sure, geometrical figures, such as lines, planes, and shapes, in things. The moon appears to us as a circle; the border of a shadow cast by a cloud on a hillside is a geometric plane made visible; the boundaries of everyday objects are so many lines. The geometer's interest, however, is more abstract, more universal. She wants to know what makes a circle a circle, and how best we may capture in words just what that nature is. To the geometer, it makes all the difference in the world whether we say the circle is a set of points or a plane figure bounded by one line. If the imagination were the final arbiter in geometry, either account would suffice. We can easily imagine a circle to be a whole composed of tiny parts, each of them gently and uniformly curved so that, when they are fit together in the right order, the proper shape results. To the geometer's ability to reason, however, such an account would not only be incoherent—she could immediately ask what happens to a tiny part should we cut it in half—but would also frustrate her ability to link one geometrical truth to the next. The tangent would no longer have its distinctive properties if it were not the intersection of a line and a circle at a single point without any length and thus without any curve.

It could be that many of us find it difficult to summon up much interest in the truth about circles. There are, however, countless truths in which we do invest ourselves, and deeply. There is no need to go looking for the perfect example, because the general features of our attachment to truth are evident from the fact that none of us appreciates being lied to, contradicted, or considered ignorant. And the subject matter of the dispute or disclosure makes hardly any difference to us. How often do we overhear or perhaps even participate in an argument about a matter of fact that could be settled in a fraction of a second by a Google search? How utterly ordinary and everyday are arguments between two people about what they have just seen or heard, and yet how often do such arguments become animated and even mean-spirited? How much damage can be done by a false statement, said purposefully and subsequently defended?

With regrettable instances such as these in mind, it should be simple enough to recognize that we regularly, even habitually, make an estimate of someone according to how he stands toward the truth. A crucial part of being a reliable person is to choose our words carefully and to describe the features of the world accurately. Whether the pitch was a ball or a strike could determine the outcome of a game. Whether an action is reported as an instance of insubordination or of healthy conflict makes the difference between a colleague's losing or keeping a job. The enormous collaborative enterprise of modern science is founded entirely and irreducibly upon the veracity of testimony about features of the world disclosed by our instruments and experiments. In all these cases, there is a moral element as well as a sensory and intellectual one. Yet we are even more alive to the good of truthfulness when what is at stake is nothing other than the disclosure of our interior state. The difference between "I love you" said sincerely and the same words said duplicitously can determine the happiness or sorrow of an entire life.

It is for this reason that the moral character of a human being is so intimately tied up with our intellectual power. If we are to be happy, we will be happy as thinking and knowing beings, and in no other way. There is no denying that we human beings live in the kingdom of truth. The correspondence of the thoughts in our minds with the way things are is no trivial matter. It is the most consequential matter of all.

To affirm this truth about truth is to be somewhat out of step with the prevailing culture of secular modernity. We can hardly fail to notice that modernity prides itself on being rational. Yet the rationality with which modernity satisfies itself is instrumental reason, a use of the mind's power as a tool or mechanism for accomplishing our will and satisfying our sense appetites. This feature of modernity is apparent both in our artistic culture and in our use of technology, areas of modern culture that are fast converging and becoming unified. The consumption of entertainment, usually through some technological device rather than live and in person, is increasingly regarded as value neutral, as though the good to be sought were simply stimulation, regardless of the content or implicit truth claims conveyed.

Today it is common to expose ourselves to ideas and pay attention to their dramatic enactment without evaluating their truth or falsity. Long ago, St. Augustine recognized this possibility, lamenting his habitual attachment to the stimulation he received at the theater. Artistic expressions are, to be sure, not the same as scientific or philosophical discourses, and they cannot always be reduced into simple propositions. Nevertheless, artistic works express a perspective on the truth, and we do ourselves a disservice if we seek only to experience the emotions evoked by a story, a Gothic cathedral, or a classical sculpture, without also asking whether such artistic expressions communicate something true about human nature, human relationships, or God.

Rationality in its fullest sense aims not at power but at truth; the fullness of reason does not merely try to manipulate ideas to achieve comfort or momentary relief from boredom; it tries to apprehend reality, to understand things as they are, and to know and to say what is true. Even in the mundane sciences, truths about physical reality in some sense transcend physical reality, and can thereby lift our attention to higher and even more transcendent truth, to the origin of all truths in Truth itself.

Yes, the Christian Faith also makes truth claims. Worship is not merely a therapeutic practice. In fact, worship has a therapeutic effect only on the soul of a person who takes seriously its claims of truth. One of the features of modernity is that the temptation to diminish truth claims into mere opinions has infected even sincerely religious people, who describe their beliefs as "personal" or "private" and conceive of them as more a matter of feelings and emotion than as true claims about reality. It is true that religious belief is personally felt and helps shape our affections, but it can do so only if the claims of religious belief are taken seriously as expressions of truth. God exists. God loves you. He has shown you the Way of salvation. These are dramatic assertions, but if they are not *true*, they can have no effective meaning, personal or otherwise.

St. Augustine's Thirst for Truth

Benedict XVI

As a child he learned the Catholic faith from Monica, his mother. But he abandoned this faith as an adolescent because he could no longer discern its reasonableness and rejected a religion that was not, to his mind, also an expression of reason, that is, of the truth. His thirst for truth was radical and therefore led him to drift away from the Catholic faith. Yet his radicalism was such that he could not be satisfied with philosophies that did not go to the truth itself, that did not go to God and to a God who was not only the ultimate cosmological hypothesis but the true God, the God who gives life and enters into our lives.

Thus, Augustine's entire intellectual and spiritual development is also a valid model today in the relationship between faith and reason, a subject not only for believers but for every person who seeks the truth, a central theme for the balance and destiny of every human being.[64]

---

[64] Benedict XVI, "Saint Augustine of Hippo (3)," General Audience, January 30, 2008.

Truthful

Questions for Reflection

• *Do I cultivate a desire not only to experience things, but to know and understand their natures, to grasp the truth of things?*

• *In my speech, do I strive for precise, careful phrasing, to communicate clearly the concepts I intend and the truths I mean to assert?*

• *When I see a movie or read a novel, do I go beyond appreciating whether the story is compelling, and ask whether or to what degree it is true?*

15

Reasonable

Wisdom is a fountain of life.

—Proverbs 16:22

Reasoning about reasoning is a bit like reading about reading: it sounds paradoxical. If you can do it, you are already doing it. If you cannot do it, what good is it to try?

As it happens, more than seventy years ago Mortimer Adler wrote a book called *How to Read a Book*. Enduringly popular and profoundly useful, it found an audience because many people who knew how to read in a basic way knew that they did not know how to read as well and as thoughtfully as they should. They did not know how to read important books fruitfully; they were not confident that reading had become, for them, what Adler said it could be: "a basic tool in living a good life."[65]

Adler's advice was to emphasize that good reading is active. It is not a process of filling up the mind with information

[65] Mortimer Adler, *How to Read a Book: The Art of Getting a Liberal Education* (New York: Simon and Schuster, 1940), vii.

transferred from a book, but instead it is a strengthening of the mind by operating upon and engaging with a book. Worthy books do not merely record information; they offer wisdom, or, if not wisdom, at least ideas worth taking seriously. It takes mental work to discern and to process what a good book has to offer. Adler offered rules to help us to become active readers, rules based on the different kinds of operation the mind must make to get the most out of a book. His rules were many, but they fell into three main habits of engaging a text. The first he called structural or analytic reading; the reader begins by looking at the book as a whole and asking what it is about in general and how it is organized. His second kind of reading was interpretive or synthetic; now the reader asks what the book is saying about its chosen topic, and how it is making its case. The third type of reading was critical or evaluative; now, at last, the reader asks whether what the book is saying is true.

As Adler saw, the point of reading is to understand, and that is why his advice about reading is, in the end, advice about reasoning. Whether in conversation, in private reflection, or in any other attempt to come to rational understanding, we must analyze, interpret, and evaluate. If we are trying to address a problem, we must identify the general issue, grasp its specific nature, and size up its significance. If we are trying to make sense of a proposal, we must grasp first what it is about, then comprehend its details, and then evaluate its worth.

These essential, everyday mental acts involve reasoning, which is a movement of the mind from one truth to another. In its archetypal form, in the discourse known as the syllogism, reasoning enables us to demonstrate the truth of a proposition. We will consider an example from a venerable logic textbook. The author set as his goal to prove "that the apostles are trustworthy with respect to their testimony that they saw Jesus Christ risen from the dead." Here is his proof:

> Every disinterested witness is trustworthy;
> But the apostles are disinterested witnesses;
> Therefore, the apostles are trustworthy.[66]

This is a helpful example for two reasons. First, it is easy to appreciate the movement of the mind through the discourse. The basic claims or premises are the first two sentences; if we are convinced by them, then we are led ineluctably to affirm the conclusion, which is the third. Second, it is equally apparent that the entire force of the argument is contained in the phrase that the two premises share and that joins them together, the idea of a disinterested witness. If we understand that a disinterested witness is someone who has nothing to gain from telling an untruth, and if we are convinced that the apostles were just such men, then we are in possession of a powerful support for our faith. Reasoning, then, provides us with arguments, that is, with reasons to hold a given statement to be true or false. Reasoning also provides us with answers to questions.

It should be evident, then, that it is by reasoning that we learn many of the things that we come to know, and that it is by reasoning that we defend the truth of some of our deepest convictions.

This is why we should take care to note that authentic reasoning is much weightier and nobler than what is typically offered under the guise of critical thinking. The phrase is a buzzword in pedagogical discussions at both the secondary and collegiate

---

[66] Jacques-Bénigne Bossuet, *La Logique du Dauphin* (ca. 1675; first published in 1828).

levels, as well as in certain corporate settings. Yet what courses in critical thinking typically provide are strategies for reflection or questioning that are not actually ordered to the attainment of truth and certainly not to right moral evaluation. They are the tools of the clever skeptic who is always finding another objection or weakness in someone's reasoning. What we need much more than this sort of skill is an ability to think constructively and synthetically, which is what genuine rational argument provides.

Some of the most celebrated arguments of the whole career of human thought are the five ways by which St. Thomas Aquinas demonstrated the existence of God early in his great work, the *Summa Theologiae*. Let us consider a simplified version of the fifth of those five ways, the argument from the order of nature to the existence of a mind that created nature. The argument was already time-honored by the time Aquinas was writing. In the fourth century, St. Gregory of Nazianzus expressed it in these terms:

> That God, the creative and sustaining cause of all, exists, sight and instinctive law informs us — sight, which lights upon things seen as nobly fixed in their courses, borne along in, so to say, motionless movement; instinctive law, which infers their author through the things seen in their orderliness. How could this universe have had foundation or constitution, unless God gave all things being and sustains them? No one seeing a beautifully elaborated lyre with its harmonious, orderly arrangement, and hearing the lyre's music will fail to form a notion of its craftsman-player, to recur to him in thought though ignorant of him by sight.[67]

[67] St. Gregory of Nazianzus, *On God and Christ: The Five Theological Orations and Two Letters to Cledonius*, trans. Lionel Wickham

Reasonable

In stark simplicity, the argument can be presented in terms of a single syllogism:

> Whatever is ordered is caused by mind.
> Nature is ordered.
> Therefore, nature is caused by mind.

When reduced to these elemental terms, it is apparent that the force of the argument turns on our understanding of order. As is the case with every word made use of by philosophers, *order* has multiple meanings. (It would be a decent, offhand definition of philosophy to say that it is the practice of trying to use with precision, and for the sake of knowing, words that admit of multiple meanings.) We think of spatial order, temporal order, or an order of causation. In whichever way we care to think about order, however, it is apparent to us that nature is so ordered. We do not expect to find an albatross in Nebraska or a grizzly bear in New York. In the northern hemisphere, snow does not usually fall in July, except perhaps in Alaska. And rabbits eat lettuce, not the other way around. The first premise is perhaps more difficult, but when we reflect upon the human experience, we see that orderliness and lawlike regularity comes from intentional human behavior rather than from the impulse of our sense appetites. Whether we are building a home, putting a sentence together, or even taking a walk around our neighborhood, it is from our mind, that is, from our intention that the orderliness of our action comes.

The key to the argument is that we are aware that rabbits do not think about what they eat, nor grizzlies and albatrosses about where they live, nor the snow when it should fall. If their

---

(Crestwood, New York: St. Vladimir's Seminary Press, 2002), 40–41.

activities happen in patterns, therefore, they must be proceeding from a mind that brings the orderliness of their action into being. And that mind is God's.

Here two opposing trains of thought present themselves.

The first, and in one sense the better consideration, goes something like this: *What a lovely argument, lovely both because of its appealing simplicity and because its conclusion is so congenial. The world is indeed a beautifully ordered place, and one simply cannot conceive of its beautiful order as being anything other than the product of mind, the mind of the God who brought the whole universe into being out of nothing for no reason other than to share his goodness with creatures.*

The second thought brings a furrow to the brow and may have a shape like the following: *I want to accept this argument. That is, I see that the argument works, so long as the premises are true. But I am having a hard time with those premises, because I have heard so many people say that the world is a product of chance and that the orderliness of living things is the result of an evolutionary process that is haphazard and kept moving forward only by the pressure of natural selection.*

Both sequences of thoughts are, in their own ways, eminently sensible. Let us take up the second one first. Aquinas once said something about the manner in which we learn things that should be both illuminating and consoling in this regard. "To understand," he wrote, "it is necessary that those things that a man hears become, as it were, connatural to him in order that they may be impressed perfectly on his mind. For this a man needs time in which his intellect may be confirmed in what it has received, by much meditation."[68] In other words, to attain a clear

[68] St. Thomas Aquinas, *Commentary on Aristotle's Nicomachean Ethics* no. 1344, trans. C. I. Litzinger, O.P. (Notre Dame, IN: Dumb Ox Books, 1993).

understanding and firm conviction about a principle such as the claim "nature is ordered" is not the work of an instant. Indeed, it may be the work of a lifetime.

Gabriel Marcel said it well when he argued that the metaphor of a journey is overused in philosophy. We should instead, he contended, think of the search for truth as being similar to the work of a gardener. He asked us to consider the philosophical search for truth to be like "a certain clearing of the ground ... of which the successful results can never be considered as finally consolidated. There is always a risk that weeds will spread in the furrows that have been so laboriously plowed, there will always be swarms of pestilent insects to threaten future harvests." For this reason, he concluded, the philosopher must bring to his work a "constant vigilance which cannot be relaxed without compromising everything."[69]

Reasoning, clearly, is not exhausted by the formal demonstration rules of valid deductive logic. Reasoning depends on some principles that cannot be demonstrated, and it is one of the classic beginner's mistakes of philosophy to expect everything to be provable. The harder work of philosophy (as in science) is the discovery of truths by indirect inquiry. The formulation of a hypothesis is a work of reason, as is its testing by dialectical investigation. Reasoning includes, then, not only identifying syllogistic forms, but imagining test cases and counterexamples, discerning analogies and metaphors, testing alternative narratives, and envisioning alternative perspectives. Knowing when it is appropriate to expect proof is an act of reason, as is recognizing the circumstances in which rationality includes deference to

[69] Gabriel Marcel, "Value and Immortality" (1943) in *Homo Viator* (South Bend, IN: St. Augustine's Press, 2010), 128–129.

tradition and authority, to conventional wisdom or communal insight.

Today, more than ever, we need to be aware that we will not attain the truth, that is, the steady possession of the knowledge of God, by stumbling into it or receiving it as a sudden and unexpected inheritance. No, if we want to understand the natures of things and to be able to defend our convictions with reasons, we will need to work. The peace attained by philosophy, by reasoning, is a peace that is attained through vigilance. An enormous part of that vigilance, as we have seen, is keeping a firm hold on our appetitive and sensory lives, so that our minds are free of vain illusions and apt to grasp the being of things as they are. The mind is a very delicate lens, and if we want it to receive illumination—to borrow Plato's metaphor—we must be vigilant in keeping it safe from being scratched and warped.

For all that, however, the first train of thought, the one that welcomed the reasoning to a divine intelligence, is not wrong. In fact, the argument is perfectly valid and its premises are absolutely true, even though coming to an adequate understanding of them may require years of reflection. (And to provide an adequate defense of the argument would require a book longer and considerably more difficult than this one.[70]) That this should be so is no great surprise. The human mind, after all, is well proportioned to its principal tools—the senses generally and our hands in particular—and to its chief work, which is to keep us alive through the works of what may broadly be called art or technology. Accordingly, we find it easiest to think through

---

[70] We recommend Michael Augros, *Who Designed the Designer? A Rediscovered Path to God's Existence* (San Francisco: Ignatius Press, 2015).

problems such as how to finance an automobile purchase or how to put together a desk from Ikea. Proving the existence of God or the immortality of the soul, however, takes us well beyond the senses. These are not everyday endeavors, and they are certainly not easy arguments. It is because the conclusions that such proofs offer are so very worthy and weighty that we do not expect the arguments to be easy, nor do we expect the glib atheists of our day to be successful in their attempts to disprove them. We know that the wise who have gone before us and who stand to us as teachers and masters offer us their wisdom as a path to follow. Their reasoning may take us decades of vigilant labor to master, but we will be made more reasonable only by the effort.

The Thought of God

Blessed John Henry Newman

I say, then, that the happiness of the soul consists in the exercise of the affections; not in sensual pleasures, not in activity, not in excitement, not in self-esteem, not in the consciousness of power, not in knowledge; in none of these things lies our happiness, but in our affections being elicited, employed, supplied. As hunger and thirst, as taste, sound, and smell, are the channels through which this bodily frame receives pleasure, so the affections are the instruments by which the soul has pleasure. When they are exercised duly, it is happy; when they are undeveloped, restrained, or thwarted, it is not happy. This is our real and true bliss, not to know, or to affect, or to pursue; but to love, to hope, to joy, to admire, to revere, to adore. Our real and true bliss lies in the possession of those objects on which our hearts may rest and be satisfied. Now, if this be so, here is at once a reason for saying that the thought of God, and nothing short of it, is the happiness of man; for though there is much besides to serve as subject of knowledge, or motive for action, or means of excitement, yet the affections require a something more vast and more enduring than anything created. What is novel and sudden excites, but does not influence; what is pleasurable or useful raises no awe; self moves no reverence, and mere knowledge kindles no love. He alone is sufficient for the heart.[71]

Questions for Reflection

- *Have I been reading this book attentively and energetically, that is, attempting to follow in my own mind the movement of reason that it contains?*

- *Am I patient and hopeful in the face of contemporary objections to the teaching of the Church and to the truths of nature, remembering that arguments in support of my deepest convictions are not lacking, even if I have myself not mastered them?*

- *Have I been complacent or vigilant in the pursuit and cultivation of truth?*

[71] John Henry Newman, "The Thought of God the Stay of the Soul," *Parochial and Plain Sermons*, V:315–316.

16

Decisive

*Reason is the beginning of every work, and coun-
sel precedes every undertaking.*

—Sirach 37:16

Quick! You must make a decision. How are you going to do it?

The question is not quite fair. Before knowing how to make a decision, we must know what it is a decision about. Is it a decision about which home to buy, or about what to have for lunch? Is it a decision about what to wear to the party, or about whether to consider a change of careers? Before any decision, we must know what is at stake and what options are available to address it.

So, we must understand the problem and then consider its possible solutions. Yet even this is too simplistic. Decision-making draws on a surprisingly complex array of mental energy and attention. Understanding the problem is a matter of sense awareness, imagination, perception, experience, and rational thought. We even have some choice in how we formulate the problem before we solve it. Considering options to solve the problem also draws on the same faculties—sensory and intellectual—to anticipate possible outcomes, recognize constraints, not to mention further powers of evaluation to weigh the benefits and costs, both material and moral.

Our reflection on decisiveness comes near the end of this book precisely because it draws on so many levels of human awareness. It is also because it is our decisions that cause the actions that build the habits that constitute our character. Who we are, and what we will be, is determined by our decisions.

The great burden of human life, but also the great blessing, is making choices. God's gift to us is a share in His providence: we have a hand in how things will go, for us and for those around us.

Given what is at stake, perhaps we should not be surprised about how adept we can be at agonizing over and avoiding choices. We procrastinate. We overthink. We look for ways to put responsibility on someone else by passing the buck, or, like the weak manager, by refusing to own a decision by blaming the constraints of bureaucracy. Psychologically, we can even experience the proliferation of options as a paralysis of the ability to choose. Even when we do decide, we can fail to follow through or to keep a resolution, or we can be overwhelmed with self-doubt and second-guessing.

The ways decision-making can fail or falter have given rise to a number of attempts to shore up this basic human function. Educators have shown an interest in identifying grit or cultivating a growth mind-set. Some self-help experts posit cultivating a systems approach instead of a goals approach, or they invite us to focus on the question of who we want to be, rather than what we want to do. Companies seek decisive leaders (even as they also want leaders who are good listeners responsive to our concerns), and a questionable industry in leadership training promises to help develop the skill of decision-making.

Alas, there is no quick path to decisiveness. It is neither a raw personality trait nor a discrete skill. Decisiveness gets at what, in the classical tradition, was addressed under the auspices of prudence, or practical wisdom. This is the fundamental and overarching virtue of good judgment. Its effect is the decision itself, but as we have seen, if the decision is to be the right one, it must be preceded by a complex capacity for thought integrated with a disciplined and developed heart.

Following Aristotle and Aquinas, we can identify four elements of practical wisdom, or prudence. First, it requires a kind of general knowledge of the relevant principles of action. A person cannot be prudent without awareness of eternal moral verities that must guide all action. Second, prudence involves the ability to apply such general practical knowledge to particular circumstances. It is one thing to recognize the object on the ground as a wallet; it is another to know that this is a case of finding lost property that ought to be restored to its rightful owner. Third, prudence involves a well-habituated will, that is, virtue. After all, the vicious person might recognize the wallet as lost property and know in an abstract sense that it ought to be restored to its rightful owner. But the unjust person is not inclined to restore it. He is at least tempted to keep any valuable contents. Only the just person is already oriented to act well when he recognizes lost property.

Finally, prudence involves the ability to reason well about how to achieve a determined end. This is deliberation. Often the focal point of practical reasoning, without the other elements of prudence the art of deliberation would be mere cleverness in satisfying desires. Only when it is accompanied by the right orientation of the will and the knowledge and application of moral principles is effective deliberation virtuous. It is thus with the assumption of this larger context of virtue that calculation of means to an end, the art of deliberation, will be our special concern here.

If we have accurately perceived the thing upon which we may act and the circumstances in which we find ourselves, then it is time to deliberate about our choice of actions. A risk of deliberation is that it is potentially infinite in duration. We have probably all once or twice felt like Hamlet, "sickl'ied o'er with the pale cast of thought," incapable of making a decision because caught in the paralysis of analysis. What makes deliberation successfully result in action is connecting the particular thing or occasion that is right there in front of us to our last end.

Yet if it is seeing the end in the means that makes us decisive, we are confronted with an additional problem, because the end—the love of God and neighbor—only occasionally presents itself to us immediately. Indeed, much of the time, it is difficult for us to see how the decision before us relates to the love of God and neighbor. That is where the reasoning part of practical reasoning comes in. One way to think about practical reasoning is as a string of syllogisms or arguments that connect the means before us to our last end, with each new argument giving a better reason for or against a course of action.

Let us take an example. You are a guest at the wedding of the daughter of your closest friends. The question confronting you is whether to drink a glass of champagne in honor of the bride and groom. This may seem an odd example for practical reasoning. After all, a variety of good habits, or virtues, would make the decision almost automatic. You are accustomed to drinking wine at the right time, for the right reasons, and in the right amount, and you are also accustomed to gratitude and friendliness. Without further ado, then, you accept the glass, raise it, and cheer.

That is exactly right. Implicit in this almost instantaneous action, however, is a course of practical reasoning that might go something like this. You enjoy wine, and this thing before you is a glass of it. Already you have a reason to act: to quench your thirst and gain the pleasure that the wine offers. You know it is possible to drink too much, but one glass at the right time for the right reason is certainly a temperate act. Moreover, this is a special social occasion, and what you owe to your friends at this moment is to rejoice with them about the marriage of their daughter. So, to heighten the gladness of the company, you willingly participate in the toast as an act of friendship, which, as a manifestation of both justice and love, is precisely what your more personal virtue of temperance is meant to serve. You might even think of Jesus, contributing to the celebration at Cana at his Mother's intercession, and so with your glass held high, your toast to the married couple is also a thanksgiving to God.

What we see here is the order of goods, from private, sensible goods through spiritual goods that are more and more common, ending with the love of God as the highest good. In its own limited way, then, a celebratory glass becomes an act of worship, an act of thanksgiving. This imaginary course of practical reasoning has been eminently successful, for it led to decisive action that made us grateful and at peace. To be sure, we rarely need to think through every action in our lives with a course of reasons that ties them down to the love of God as their last end. In the case of our wedding toast, such reasoning may need to be articulated to oneself only if there is some obstacle, a threat of interruption. Perhaps you are at risk of being distracted by worries—an impending work obligation or a personal illness—and so not otherwise in a mood to celebrate. In such case, brief reflection might help gain perspective on your worries, and refocus your awareness of the obligations of the moment.

Even when not consciously articulated, what is essential is merely that our actions be in conformity with what that reasoning would indicate if it were made explicit. If our hearts are well tuned and our minds are clear about our true good, our actions will be nearly seamless, and the reasoning that is implicit behind our choices will often recede from conscious view. That is the power of virtue, and especially of the virtue of practical wisdom. What the world sees is not the cogs and wheels of thoughts churning, but gracious, good, and decisive action.

The example of the wedding toast is a simple example of a discrete decision, but it points to principles that can be relevant to every decision, including those life-changing decisions that lead to things like weddings. The challenge of discerning a vocation is, in the end, a matter of making a decision. True, we hope that God will lead us, and show us our particular path, but God will not do this without our participation, without our choosing the path. True, a vocation or "calling" might be experienced as a being chosen, rather than an individual choice, but even this being chosen will work in and through our own will, our receptiveness to promptings, and our willing consent to hear and follow God's call. Mary's yes is a receptive surrender, but it was also a discernment and decision, made possible by a life intently and deliberately ordered to God.

At this point, however, you may be inclined to protest. It is all well and good, you might say, to analyze how we might go about reasoning about what to do — either internally or, perhaps more likely, with the counsel of a friend to help us think the matter through — but the hard part remains, which is to do the deed. The point is an essential one, for practical wisdom or prudence is a hybrid virtue. We have just been talking about what it accomplishes for us in terms of reasoning, but it also enables us to act, and to act involves the will.

As the appetite of reason, the will is often hidden from our view. We do not doubt that we have one, but we also know that we do not feel it the way we do our appetite for food. Any time we choose a course of action against what our sense appetites would have us do—as, for instance, when we stay up late to finish an assignment or fast on Good Friday—our will wins the victory. Conversely, any time we know what we ought to do but fail to do it, our will bears the burden of defeat.[72]

Because we are social beings, it is natural and right for our will to receive strength from friends and trusted authorities. Especially in difficult decisions, it is important to take the interior conversation you might have with yourself into a real conversation with others, seeking their counsel. We can often receive new perspective and encouragement from others, and even the task of articulating a difficulty to others can help us to clarify and bring order to our thoughts. The prudent person does not resist advice and counsel, but seeks it out, and his will is strengthened by exercising it with others—the counsel of friends, and in prayer, the counsel of God.

The road to a stronger will does not come to an end in this life, and it is strewn with rude obstacles and bitter disappointments. Yet there is good news. God created us as free beings and instilled in our wills a love of the good. The human will is

---

[72] For an excellent discussion of the will, as well as a luminous presentation of the life of the virtues, see Steven J. Jensen, *Living the Good Life: A Beginner's Thomistic Ethics* (Washington, DC: Catholic University of America Press, 2013).

already in motion from the moment of its creation by God, and the impetus that it receives is oriented back to him as its end. Moreover, just as the soul is the life of the body, so also God is the life of our soul. His grace is at work deep within, offering countless inspirations to recognize the good and to choose it. Our freedom is a gift beyond price. God's grace does not compel but acts upon our souls by strengthening, sharpening, and directing our own native ability to choose. Relying on God's grace, then, does not mean that we are absolved from making a decision: quite the contrary. As St. Irenaeus of Lyons said, "the glory of God is the living man" (*Gloria enim Dei vivens homo*). Were he alive today, he might tell us that God could have made us into robots or puppets had he wished, but that he plainly did not wish to do so. God created us to live, that is, to discover the right course of action and to choose it. Grounded in the counsel of trusted friends and in a trusting confidence in Divine Providence, we can indeed become decisive men and women who thoughtfully and confidently pursue the good that lies before us every day, ordering our every action—however trivial it may be in itself—to serve the glory of God and the salvation of souls.

Trusting in God's Providence

Blessed John Henry Newman

God has created me to do him some definite service; he has committed some work to me which he has not committed to another. I have my mission—I may never know it in this life, but I shall be told it in the next. Somehow I am necessary for his purposes, as necessary in my place as an archangel in his—if, indeed, I fail, God can raise another, as he could make the stones children of Abraham. Yet I have a part in this great work; I am a link in a chain, a bond of connection between persons. He has not created me for naught.

I shall do good. I shall do his work. I shall be an angel of peace, a preacher of truth in my own place, though not intending it, if I do but keep his commandments and serve him in my calling.

Therefore I will trust him. Whatever, wherever I am, I can never be thrown away. If I am in sickness, my sickness may serve him; in perplexity, my perplexity may serve him; if I am in sorrow, my sorrow may serve him. My sickness, or perplexity, or sorrow may be necessary causes of some great end, which is quite beyond us. He does nothing in vain. He may prolong my life; he may shorten it. He knows what he is about. He may take away my friends. He may throw me among strangers. He may make me feel desolate, make my spirits sink, hide the future from me — still he knows what he is about.[73]

Questions for Reflection

• *Do I allow myself to become paralyzed by overthinking choices I face?*

• *Am I consistent in seeking counsel from friends and trusted advisers who can help me order my actions to their ultimate end and my highest good: the love of God and neighbor?*

[73] John Henry Newman, *Everyday Meditations* (Manchester, NH: Sophia Institute Press, 2013), 8–9.

A Mind at Peace

• *Do I pray for God's grace before I make important decisions and begin important tasks, confident that God's sole desire is my eternal happiness and the well-being and eternal salvation of those I serve?*

17

Wise

The person to whom all things are one and who re-
fers all things to one and sees all things in one is able
to be steadfast and to remain at peace in God.

—Thomas à Kempis, *The Imitation of Christ* I.3

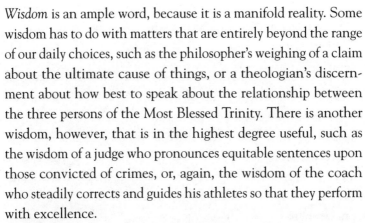

Wisdom is an ample word, because it is a manifold reality. Some
wisdom has to do with matters that are entirely beyond the range
of our daily choices, such as the philosopher's weighing of a claim
about the ultimate cause of things, or a theologian's discernment about how best to speak about the relationship between
the three persons of the Most Blessed Trinity. There is another
wisdom, however, that is in the highest degree useful, such as
the wisdom of a judge who pronounces equitable sentences upon
those convicted of crimes, or, again, the wisdom of the coach
who steadily corrects and guides his athletes so that they perform
with excellence.

The heights of human wisdom are difficult to describe without
already standing on them. Still, we do recognize wisdom when
we see it. Aristotle said that the wise man has a comprehensive

knowledge, especially of what is difficult and valuable, that he knows with precision and has the ability to teach, and most importantly that his knowledge gives him authority. Wisdom is knowledge that orders. John Henry Newman described the qualities of a mind habituated to wisdom:

> When the intellect has once been properly trained and formed to have a connected view or grasp of things, it will display its powers with more or less effect according to its particular quality and capacity in the individual. In the case of most men it makes itself felt in the good sense, sobriety of thought, reasonableness, candour, self-command, and steadiness of view, which characterize it. In some it will have developed habits of business, power of influencing others, and sagacity. In others it will elicit the talent of philosophical speculation, and lead the mind forward to eminence in this or that intellectual department. In all it will be a faculty of entering with comparative ease into any subject of thought, and of taking up with aptitude any science or profession.[74]

This much can be said of human wisdom. There is yet another distinction among the kinds of wisdom, a distinction of origin, for the types of wisdom just mentioned are acquired by study or through experience, whereas there is also wisdom that comes to us directly "from above" (James 3:17) as the best of the gifts of the Holy Spirit. This supernatural wisdom, which also encompasses both forms of human or acquired wisdom, is our particular concern here.

---

[74] John Henry Newman, *The Idea of a University* (Tacoma: Cluny Media, 2016), 11.

Having been given the gift of faith at baptism, and since then having received "grace upon grace" (John 1:16), we are now somewhere along life's journey to be "renewed in the spirit of our minds" (Eph. 4:23). We know that "the truth is in Jesus" (Eph. 4:21), and so we wish to conform our thoughts and desires to his. Yet herein lies a great difficulty: we know that our minds are those of creatures, but that the mind of Jesus is the mind of the eternal, omnipotent God. Our thoughts do not measure his; his measure ours. How shall we climb this holy mountain? If we are to learn the things of God, then, we must find those who can teach us how to be receptive to the inspiration of the Holy Spirit. If we would be wise, we must take ourselves to the school of the saints, to learn how to think and to love like Jesus.

A fitting model for wisdom in the twenty-first century is St. Teresa Benedicta of the Cross, the Carmelite philosopher-martyr Edith Stein. St. John Paul II proposed her to us as an "eloquent example of interior renewal."[75] She is especially helpful as an example of an interior life in which the excellences of moral virtue, studiousness, and intellectual virtue were seamlessly integrated and further transfigured by the gifts of the Holy Spirit. Edith Stein was raised in a Jewish family in the eastern part of the German Empire at the turn of the twentieth century. A brilliant but melancholy girl, she lost her faith in God while still a child and traded in the remembrances and observances cherished by her pious mother for academic pursuits. She became a philosopher—a rare achievement for a woman in those times—and by God's grace was placed in a setting in which her fellow students were reopening metaphysical questions that had been closed for the greater part of the previous century. A patriot,

[75] St. John Paul II, "Homily for the Canonization of Edith Stein."

she volunteered as a nurse during the Great War, but the deep
questions that had been raised in her mind continued to prompt
her to further study and reflection. And God, ever watchful, ever
gracious, remembered his daughter, and with three sharp twitches
on the thread of her life, pulled her close to him.

The first grace of Edith Stein's conversion came at the home
of an Evangelical Christian, the war widow of one of her mentors. When Stein went to comfort her friend for the loss of her
husband, she found the tables turned on her and herself receiving
comfort from the sorrowing wife.

> It was my first encounter with the Cross and the divine
> power that it bestows on those who carry it. For the first
> time, I was seeing with my very eyes the Church, born
> from its Redeemer's sufferings, triumphant over the sting
> of death. That was the moment my unbelief collapsed
> and Christ shone forth — in the mystery of the Cross.[76]

Now no longer an atheist, Edith continued her journey to
Christ but remained, for the moment, outside his Church. Visit-
ing a trusted friend led her a step closer. Left alone one evening
in her friend's library, Stein met St. Teresa of Avila through the
pages of her autobiography and knew immediately that she had
found a sister, a mother, and a spiritual family. From that evening,
she knew that she must become a Catholic.

By a third pull on the string, she was drawn to marvel at
the gift of the Eucharist through the simple experience of seeing a stranger make a visit to the Blessed Sacrament. "In the
synagogue," she explained, "as in the Protestant churches I had

---

[76] Waltraud Herbstrith, *Edith Stein: A Biography*, trans. Bernard
Bonowitz, O.C.D. (San Francisco: Ignatius Press, 1992), 56.

visited, people only went in at the time of the service. But here was someone coming into the empty church in the middle of a day's work as if to talk to a friend. I have never been able to forget that."[77] In each of these three defining moments of her conversion, Stein was the recipient of actual graces transmitted to her through the lives of three Christians who were docile to the promptings of the Holy Spirit. The modesty of these actions—Anna Reinach's consoling words, Hedwig Conrad-Martius's choice of books, and an unknown person's gesture of love to Jesus in the tabernacle—should not cause us to overlook their significance. Each was in its way a manifestation of the gift of wisdom; each small deed proceeded from a mind attentive to things of God.

For Edith Stein, the beneficiary of these graces, God had further plans. After her baptism, she lived as a single woman in the world, helping to train Dominican sisters to become teachers, while continuing to study philosophy and immersing herself in the works of Newman and Aquinas. Stein's correspondence with her former students reveals that she was a gifted teacher whose wisdom was appreciated even then. It is encouraging to see the humility of these Dominicans, who did not hesitate to ask advice about spiritual matters from a Carmelite and from a woman who had been a Christian for only a few years. The sisters, it seems, were able to sense that God was at work in her mind and heart and bringing her swiftly to a high degree of charity, the very cause of wisdom.

We see this wisdom and charity in a letter St. Teresa Benedicta of the Cross sent to a young girl who had sought her advice

---

[77] Ibid., 63.

in a time of disappointment and frustration. "Dear Anneliese," she began,

> God leads each of us on an individual way; one reaches the goal more easily and more quickly than another. We can do very little ourselves, compared to what is done to us. But that little bit we must do. Primarily, this consists before all else of persevering in prayer to find the right way, and of following without resistance the attraction of grace when we feel it. Whoever acts in this way and perseveres patiently will not be able to say that his efforts were in vain. But one may not set a deadline for the Lord....
>
> Obviously it is no small matter for you to return to [school]. But that is what has been decided for you, and you have no responsibility for it. Do as much as you can, and give your parents a regular account of your standing so there will be no surprise if things go badly.... Then we will see about the future. Among the books you got as a child, do you have Andersen's *Fairy Tales*? If so, read the story of the ugly duckling. I believe in your swan-destiny. Just don't hold it against others if they haven't discovered it yet, and don't let yourself become bitter. You are not the only one to make mistakes day after day—we all do it. But the Lord is patient and full of mercy. In his household of grace he can use our faults, too, if we lay them on the altar for him. *Cor contritum et humiliatum Deus non despicies.* That, too, is one of my favorite verses.[78]

---

[78] Sister Teresa Benedicta of the Cross, *Self-Portrait in Letters*, volume 5 of *The Collected Works of Edith Stein*, trans. Josephine Koeppel, O.C.D. (Washington, DC: ICS Publications, 1993),

Wise

These lovely words of consolation and guidance are a window onto the wisdom of a saint. In these few lines we see the full amplitude of Christian wisdom: insight into the things of God that has been won by the labor of study, an ability to give good counsel that has been honed by long experience and suffering borne lovingly for Christ's sake, and a sense of the right medicine to apply that has been gained by prayerful attentiveness to the Holy Spirit. And it is also an everyday wisdom, practical and effective. This is the kind of wisdom that will help us not only to secure our peace of mind but also to be agents of peace for others.

If any of you lacks wisdom, let him ask God, who gives
to all men generously and without reproaching,
and it will be given him. (James 1:5)

Solomon's Prayer for Wisdom

See Wisdom 9:1–6, 9–10

O God of my fathers and Lord of mercy, who have made all things by your word, and by your wisdom have formed man, to have dominion over the creatures you have made, and rule the world in holiness and righteousness, and pronounce judgment in uprightness of soul, give me the wisdom that sits by your throne, and do not reject me from among your servants. For I am your slave and the son of your maidservant, a man who is weak and short-lived, with little understanding of judgment and laws; for

---

100–101. The Latin phrase is from Ps. 51:17: "A broken and contrite heart, O God, thou wilt not despise."

even if one is perfect among the sons of men, yet without the wisdom that comes from you he will be regarded as nothing.

With you is wisdom, who knows your works and was present when you made the world, and who understands what is pleasing in your sight and what is right according to your commandments. Send her forth from the holy heavens, and from the throne of glory send her, that she may be with me and toil, and that I may learn what is pleasing to you.

Questions for Reflection

• *Do I have close friends among the saints whose example I follow and whose intercession I seek?*

• *Do I recognize that there are those who depend on me for wise counsel and example?*

• *Do I pray for the gift of wisdom, that I might see the world as Christ does?*

18

Humble

A broken and contrite heart, O God, thou wilt not despise.

—Psalm 51:17

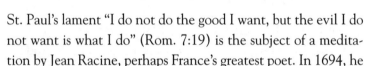

St. Paul's lament "I do not do the good I want, but the evil I do not want is what I do" (Rom. 7:19) is the subject of a meditation by Jean Racine, perhaps France's greatest poet. In 1694, he recited it before a royal audience.

> My God, what bitter strife!
> Two men I find within.
> One, full of love for thee,
> Wishes my heart ever faithful.
> The other, a rebel to your will,
> Turns me against your law.
>
> One, all spirit and supernal,
> Heavenly bound,
> Drawn by eternal gifts,
> Commands me hold the world for naught.

The other, by a deadly weight,
Bends me, bowed low, to earth.

Alas! From this war within,
Where shall I find peace?
I will, but do not act.
I will, but, O great sorrow!
I fail to do the good I love,
Yet do the wrong I hate.

O grace, with your healing rays,
Come, unify my heart;
Tame with your easy yoke
This man so set against you,
Make into your willing slave
This man enslaved to death.[79]

When Racine had finished, Louis XIV leaned over to his wife and said, "Madame, here are two men I know well."[80] And so, doubtless, do we all. Racine's poem, as the Sun King seems to have recognized, takes us to the very center of the task of self-knowledge and humility, the work of admitting that we are guilty of sin.

It is a grim task, but an essential and salutary one. Without coming to terms with sin, that is, without acknowledging our guilt, making a firm resolution to amend our lives, and imploring God's grace and mercy, we will make no lasting progress

---

[79] Jean Racine, "*Plainte d'un Chrétien sur les contrariétés qu'il éprouve au dedans de lui-même*," *Cantiques spirituels* [1694] in *Oeuvres complètes*, ed. Raymond Picard (Paris: Gallimard, 1950), I:999–1000.

[80] The story was told by Racine's son. See Louis Racine, *Vie de Racine* (1747; Paris: Les Belles Lettres, 1999), 128–129.

toward interior peace. Humility, as the great Francis de Sales taught, "is true knowledge and voluntary acknowledgement of our abjection."[81] To make a genuine act of repentance, even about a relatively small matter, a venial sin, is to take a firm hold upon the next rung of the ladder and to draw closer to God, closer to peace. Again, de Sales: "In the single act of confession you will exercise more virtues than in any other act whatsoever."[82] There is tremendous consolation here and good human wisdom. One of the most powerful passages of C. S. Lewis's *Mere Christianity* is when he considers the same problem from the opposite vantage point:

> There is one vice of which no man in the world is free; which everyone in the world loathes when he sees it in someone else; and of which hardly any people, except Christians, ever imagine that they are guilty themselves. I have heard people admit that they are bad-tempered, or that they cannot keep their heads about girls or drink, or even that they are cowards. I do not think I have ever heard anyone who was not a Christian accuse himself of this vice. And at the same time I have very seldom met anyone, who was not a Christian, who showed the slightest mercy to it in others. There is no fault which makes a man more unpopular, and no fault which we are more unconscious of in ourselves. And the more we have it ourselves, the more we dislike it in others.[83]

[81] De Sales, *Introduction to the Devout Life*, 128.
[82] Ibid., 101.
[83] C. S. Lewis, *Mere Christianity* (New York: Macmillan, 1943), 108–109.

A Mind at Peace

The fault in question is pride. Its antidote is humility, the acts of which are genuine, unflinching self-knowledge and the confession of our sins.

There are many benefits of humility, including a clear understanding of who we really are and what our duties consist in, but the greatest one may well be interior peace. The first truth of our lives is that we are creatures, made by an all-knowing and all-loving God, and the humility we exercise when we accept that we are not in charge is a necessary and effective step on the road to equanimity. The second truth surely is that we are fallen creatures, and when a humble acknowledgment of our own sin leads us to forgive others — and from the heart — then we are on the right path to interior peace, as all the great spiritual writers though the ages have taught.

At this, the last stage of our journey of self-examination and resolve, we have arrived at the hardest step, the death to self that humility requires. We have been preparing for this step all along. Pride, or self-love, is the root of every sin and of every disorder in our lives; humility and charity are what our souls always need. The first stage of our journey required us to think about our actions, and our desires to be comfortable, to acquire, and to enjoy. Even a moment's honest self-examination reveals to us that we were born into a web of relationships and duties and that each season in our lives has seen those relationships multiply and those duties deepen. There are many who rely on us. We owe it to them, for the love of God, to watch over our freedom and to direct it into right paths, into paths of genuine service and nobility.

To do this, we must bring healing to our sensory lives, which was the task of the second stage of our journey. The messages brought to us by our digital media often threaten to lead us astray by distracting us from our duty and tempting us to give in to momentary and irrational desires. Our habits of using digital media, irrespective of the content of its messages, shape our sensory lives, and very deeply. If we are honest with ourselves — that is, humble — then we will admit that our smartphones and other devices and screens are sufficiently powerful to leave us distracted, prey to whims, and, at times, thoughtless. We must resolve to be masters of our tools and not to be mastered by them because those who depend on us need us to be attentive, watchful, creative, and perceptive, and thus able to assist them by our experience. "Pride goes before destruction, and a haughty spirit before a fall," we read in Proverbs 16:18. The attraction of digital media is very powerful, because its attraction is exercised upon the two windows of the world through which our spiritual lives are most immediately engaged, our sight and our hearing. We can tell ourselves that we are immune to its temptations, just as in the past we may have told ourselves that we were immune to other kinds of temptations. Yet that would not seem to be the path of wisdom or true self-knowledge.

The third and last stage of our journey has been an examination of the mind itself, the marvelous spark of divinity that each of us bears within. We have seen that our minds are not like those of the angels. Angels were created knowing and wise; we must earn our knowledge and wisdom at great cost of study and labor, and by prayerful attentiveness to the promptings of the Holy Spirit. Everything that is in our minds comes to us through our senses, so if our sensory lives are damaged, our minds will also be. And if our minds are at risk from our habitual use of digital media, then our humanity is at risk. Yet our minds always remain open to truth, and our wills are always free to choose the good. Therein lies hope. We cannot see the future, but it seems likely that the world to be inhabited by our children and grandchildren will be more and not less influenced by the kinds of tools that today we refer to as communications devices and digital media. Our children and grandchildren will need to be strengthened in mind and heart so as not to be overmastered by them.

We are living through a great transition, a great social experiment, and a great test of human virtue and happiness. At this moment, our society is fortunate enough to have within it many men and women who can remember a time before the digital revolution, that is, a time of the possibilities of attention, imagination, and reason without the temptations of constant connectivity. These temptations are widely recognized, but not fully accounted for or explained. The work of psychologists, neuroscientists, sociologists, and cognitive theorists will continue, and, we may hope, will greatly help future generations to navigate the complexities of the digital ecosystem. For our part, we have attempted to convey some of the principles and insights that the classical and Christian tradition of wisdom about human nature offers to that work. We have done so because we are convinced that if we and our children are to use the new tools of our age for the good—retaining clear and powerful minds built upon attentive and healthy sensory lives and well-ordered moral lives—then we must take the necessary steps to correct our habits of using these tools and to cultivate wisdom. The love of God and neighbor call us to this task of self-knowledge and self-restraint. We may trust that God will grant us the graces we need for the work; it remains for us to receive those graces with humble, creaturely hearts.

> Gold is tested in fire, and acceptable men in
> the furnace of humiliation. (Sir. 2:5)

Humble

A Prayer for Divine Illumination

Blessed John Henry Newman

Come, O my dear Lord, and teach me day by day, according to each day's opportunities and needs. Give me the gift of discriminating between true and false in all discourse of mind. And, for that end, give me, O my Lord, that purity of conscience which alone can receive, which alone can improve your inspirations. My ears are dull, so that I cannot hear your voice. My eyes are dim, so that I cannot see your tokens. You alone can quicken my hearing, and purge my sight, and cleanse and renew my heart. Teach me, like Mary, to sit at your feet, and to hear your word. Give me that true wisdom which seeks your will by prayer and meditation, by direct communion with you, more than by reading and reasoning. Give me the discernment to know your voice from the voices of strangers, and to rest upon it and to seek it in the first place, as something external to myself; and answer me through my own mind, if I worship and rely on you as above and beyond it.[84]

Questions for Reflection

• *Do I acknowledge with humble realism that I am a sinner, even in small ways and in my less-than-saintly uses of everyday technology?*

[84] Newman, *Everyday Meditations*, 101–102.

A Mind at Peace

- *Have I set reasonable and sustainable limits to my use of smartphones and other digital media, limits set in light of charity's demands upon me, as accurately and honestly as I can possibly understand them?*

- *Am I accountable to others for this resolution?*

Afterword

The Peace Beyond

Be still, and know that I am God.

—Psalm 46:10

The three main sections of this book describe the work of achieving interior peace. While we have surveyed the range of the soul's powers and virtues, our purpose has been to help order the lower powers and virtues (of bodily appetites, and exterior and interior senses) in service of the higher (the properly intellectual)—not only because they are the higher, but because the modern condition poses particular challenges to the mind's discipline and peace.

The work of achieving this peace assumes the help of God's grace but, by its nature, depends on and is an achievement of human effort. We have thus striven for practical advice and encouragement. But there is another level of interior peace that is entirely dependent on God, with no role for human effort except in preparation and a humble disposition to receive the gift. We wish to address a few words to this gift of peace, this peace beyond.

We do so with some trepidation. Even a few words might perhaps be too many for a peace not only beyond human effort but beyond human words. Classical philosophy and the Christian tradition agree that the ultimate perfection of the human soul is a kind of transcendent contact with, and participation in, the perfect activity of the divine mind. The activity of God's mind is pure, and simple, and full — God's thought is his life and is the full activity of God Himself. God's mind is Divinity itself.

It is the human mind, and human language, that makes us distinguish between God, and God's mind, and the activity of God's mind. Yet if these three, divided in human thought and words, are one, then to participate in the divine life is somehow for the human mind to be lifted beyond its memory and experience, beyond discursive reasoning, arguments and inquiry, beyond assent and denial and distinction of subject and predicate, beyond even its finite concepts. The most traditional metaphor for such a state is the visual *gaze*. As the eye can stop searching and distinguishing, and simply rest in apprehending its object — in wonder, in appreciation, and in a certain unity with the object gazed upon — so the mind, brought beyond thinking *about* God, may silently gaze upon him.

Since we must have words even for the wordless, we can follow tradition and call this intellectual gaze *contemplation*. The word will sound too dry and abstract for what is essentially spiritual communion. Even in the philosophical tradition, contemplation is both a supremely rational self-realization and a loss of self beyond reason. Plato and Aristotle both describe contemplation as an activity of supreme nobility, a participation in divine life, accompanied by "pleasures marvelous for their purity and enduringness,"[85] which is perhaps too high for human beings in

---

[85] Aristotle, *Nicomachean Ethics* X.7; cf. Plato, *Republic* 585d–587a, an argument for the ordered intellect being capable of "the best and truest pleasures possible."

this life: in short, complete happiness, a wondrous gift surpassing natural human powers.

Contemplation is an intellectual perfection that is inseparable from a perfection of the heart or will. Thomas Merton said every expression of God's will is a "seed of contemplation," leading us to him by love.[86] Contemplation is thus often described in terms of burning fire, and even more personally as a lover's surrender, a spousal communion. Even Plato and Aristotle, in their own muted way, suggest that the happy man is not just a friend of truth but a lover of truth: intellect has its own *eros* seeking union with its proper object. Such a suggestion grows only stronger in the Christian tradition. St. Gregory the Great, among others, interpreted the sensual, erotic Song of Songs as an allegory for contemplation: God is a lover seeking union with the beloved.

Contemplation should be distinguished from what might be confused with it. It does not require great learning or aesthetic sensibility. It is not abstract theorizing or emotional exaltation. Nor is it numbness or ease, and while it can include delight, it does not have to and can be manifested even in and through suffering and anguish: the Dark Night of the Soul. Certainly it is not frenzy. Nor is it necessarily a cloistered, highly intellectual silence: the experience of communion with God can be had amid activity and conversation. As the perfection of the rational soul, fully activated in the presence of its transcendent object, contemplation is an activity in repose, or repose in activity, resting in the supreme life of union with God.

The superior peace is also a superior liberty, the liberty of submission to the Divine Will. As Jacques and Raïssa Maritain

[86] Thomas Merton, *New Seeds of Contemplation* (New York: New Directions, 1961), 14.

write, "Contemplation is thus the domain of the liberty of the Spirit who breathes where he wills and no man knows whence he comes or whither he goes. And it implies that the soul advancing in renunciation and detachment submits with docility to the Spirit's guidance."[87]

Spiritual writers of different temperaments and charisms emphasize different features and manifestations of contemplation, but all agree that it is rare and preceded by a difficult climb (perhaps up a ladder or a mountain). We do not need it to live a good life here below. We have no right to it. Nor do we even have a natural capacity for it: Divinity exceeds the power of our minds as the blazing sun exceeds the power of the bat's eyes. The gaze of contemplation must be infused, given as a gift by Divinity itself.

In general, those who do experience contemplation do so fleetingly, and as a foretaste of the perfect realization of the soul's union with God, available only in heaven. True contemplation is beatitude, and our ability to participate in it here and now is inherently limited and even so beyond describing. St. Augustine, relating his vision at Ostia with St. Monica, describes the before and after, but leaves the vision itself undescribed: "And while we were thus talking of His Wisdom and panting for it, with all the effort of our heart we did for one instant attain to touch it; then, sighing, and leaving the first fruits of our spirit bound to it, we returned to the sound of our own tongue, in which a word has both beginning and ending."[88]

---

[87] Jacques and Raïssa Maritain, *Prayer and Intelligence*, trans. Algar Thornold (New York: Sheed and Ward, 1942), 20.

[88] Augustine, *Confessions* IX.10, trans. Frank Sheed (Indianapolis: Hackett, 1993), 164.

Nevertheless, we are invited to seek God's wisdom, and participate in it as much as we are able. The steps of *lectio divina* move from reading, meditation, and prayer, to contemplation, with the last step, unlike the first three, more about receptivity than effort. As we use our natural powers to grow closer to God, and make ourselves more disposed to His grace, we should as much as possible make possible the undistracted leisure, the sacred interior space in which God can grant us the gift of his presence. As our highest activity, we can say that contemplation is sought for its own sake; but in another way, of course, it is sought because in it we find God. The Maritains again: "Contemplation should not be loved for its own sake but for God's. Not the joys of contemplation, but union with God through love—*that* is our end."[89]

And God does want us to achieve this. If you picked up this book and read it, you had your own good reasons for seeking peace of mind. But know this: God, too, wants you to have peace of mind. If this small volume has been a help in fulfilling your desire to reclaim order in your soul, it is only thanks to God, who himself desires it, for your sake, but also for His. In his love for you, he wishes to be known by you, and so to reclaim your soul for himself. Praise him and adore him!

> And so my mind, suspended utterly,
>> held its gaze still immobile and intent,
>> and ever kindled was my wish to see.
> Before that Light one's will to turn is spent:
>> one is so changed, it is impossible
>> to shift the glance, for one would not consent,

---

[89] Maritains, *Prayer and Intelligence*, 21.

A Mind at Peace

Because all good—the object of the will—
  is summed in it, for it alone is best:
  beyond, defective; there, whole, perfect, still.
Even for these few memories I've confessed,
  my words are less than what a baby says
  who wets his tongue still at his mama's breast,
Not that I saw more than a single face
  as I was gazing into the living glow,
  for it is ever as it ever was,
But in my vision winning valor so,
  that sole appearance as I changed by seeing
  appeared to change and form itself anew.
Within that brilliant and profoundest Being
  of the deep light three rings appeared to me,
  three colors and one measure in their gleaming:
As rainbow begets rainbow in the sky,
  so were the first two, and the third, a flame
  that from both rainbows breathed forth equally.
Alas how feeble language is, how lame
  beside my thought!—and, for what I was shown,
  to call thought "small" would be too great a claim.
O Light that dwell within Thyself alone,
  who alone know Thyself, are known, and smile
  with Love upon the Knowing and the Known![90]

[90] Dante, *Paradise*, trans. Anthony Esolen (New York: Random House, 2004), canto XXXIII, lines 97–126.

Acknowledgments

We would like to express our gratitude to those who have lent their efforts and wisdom to A *Mind at Peace*. First and foremost, our thanks to Charlie McKinney of Sophia Institute Press for his lively interest in the project since its inception. Fr. Fadi Auro, Tim Gray, Jonathan Reyes, and Edward Sri provided early counsel, encouragement, and support. Kathleen Blum, Fr. Paul Check, Paige Hochschild, Fr. Michael Keating, and Fr. Conrad Murphy read the manuscript and offered criticism that much improved it. Students in Professor Hochschild's class *Friendship and Contemplation in the Digital Age* at Mount St. Mary's University read and discussed the entire work. We thank them for thoughtful engagement; the book is stronger because of their insights and suggestions. Lastly, we each owe significant debts to family members, friends, teachers, and mentors too many to mention here. Some are still living; others have passed away; may their names all be written in the Book of Life.

Sophia Institute

Sophia Institute is a nonprofit institution that seeks to nurture the spiritual, moral, and cultural life of souls and to spread the Gospel of Christ in conformity with the authentic teachings of the Roman Catholic Church.

Sophia Institute Press fulfills this mission by offering translations, reprints, and new publications that afford readers a rich source of the enduring wisdom of mankind.

Sophia Institute also operates two popular online Catholic resources: CrisisMagazine.com and CatholicExchange.com.

Crisis Magazine provides insightful cultural analysis that arms readers with the arguments necessary for navigating the ideological and theological minefields of the day. *Catholic Exchange* provides world news from a Catholic perspective as well as daily devotionals and articles that will help you to grow in holiness and live a life consistent with the teachings of the Church.

In 2013, Sophia Institute launched Sophia Institute for Teachers to renew and rebuild Catholic culture through service to Catholic education. With the goal of nurturing the spiritual, moral, and cultural life of souls, and an abiding respect for the role and work of teachers, we strive to provide materials and programs that are at once enlightening to the mind and ennobling to the heart; faithful and complete, as well as useful and practical.

Sophia Institute gratefully recognizes the Solidarity Association for preserving and encouraging the growth of our apostolate over the course of many years. Without their generous and timely support, this book would not be in your hands.

www.SophiaInstitute.com
www.CatholicExchange.com
www.CrisisMagazine.com
www.SophiaInstituteforTeachers.org

Sophia Institute Press® is a registered trademark of Sophia Institute.
Sophia Institute is a tax-exempt institution as defined by the
Internal Revenue Code, Section 501(c)(3). Tax I.D. 22-2548708.